PRAISE FOR *THE GRUMBLE-FREE YEAR*

"Nuggets of wisdom, truth, and a whole lot of real life had me nodding my head and recognizing my own family in *The Grumble-Free Year*. This book is filled with astute observations of what is really behind our grumbling and complaining, and how we can encourage and lead our families to a more grateful Christ-filled life, starting with our own hearts and mouths."

 —Amy Roberts, author, blogger, speaker, and podcaster

"*The Grumble-Free Year* is about becoming more than just grateful. It's about learning how to see beyond the words to uncover what is really happening in the heart of our children and, equally important, ourselves. With humility and authenticity, Tricia Goyer invites us into her home to learn how to live grumble free and paints a beautiful picture of the transformation process the evolves through a steadfast commitment, even with a few detours along the way."

 —Elisa Pulliam, life coach and founder of MoretoBe.com

"When I read the title of this book, I immediately thought, *I'm out*! But then I realized that if anyone could coach me and my family to develop a deeper heart of gratitude and unity (without guilt or shame), it's Tricia. While I'd never refer to this book as a manual, it offers a beautiful mix of practicality, scripture, and personal stories to encourage anyone up for the challenge!"

 —Sami Cone, blogger, professor, and author
  of *Raising Uncommon Kids*

"I've never thought much about grumbling, nor invested much energy in an alternative approach to the daily frustrations that underlie the habit. That is, until Tricia Goyer splayed out her own challenge with grumbling in these pages. Now I'm both noticing my mumbling, bumbling grumblings and I'm learning to back up and start again in a more positive direction. Thanks Tricia—and all you brave Goyers!"

—Elisa Morgan, president emerita of MOPS International,
cohost of *Discover the Word*, speaker, and author
of *Hello, Beauty Full* and *The Prayer Coin*

"When Tricia talks, I listen. That's because whatever she writes about, she has intimately lived. But instead of presenting as a perfect expert, Tricia pulls up a chair beside you as another woman facing the same battles. *The Grumble-Free Year* is a guide that gives you practical ways to develop a practice of gratitude and to foster respect in relationships. You will feel understood, challenged, and empowered to live a grumble free lifestyle."

—Sarah Bragg, host of the podcasts *Surviving*
Sarah and *Raising Boys & Girls*

"We've become accustomed to airing our grievances and gripes privately and publicly. We receive instant rewards for grumbling with 'likes' on our Facebook posts, or with an 'Amen, sister!' from the person next to us. No wonder we've forgotten how grievous griping is. In *The Grumble-Free Year*, Tricia Goyer reminds moms and dads that grumbling isn't 'liked' or 'Amened' by God. Uh-oh. As a mom who gripes herself, I've lost sight of this and struggle to help my children curb their complaining. But after reading Tricia's insights, I've finally learned how to live with God-honoring gratitude and how to model it for my kids. Families of all sizes and stages will benefit from *The Grumble-Free Year* for its authentic experiences and practical tips that are heart-savers and home-changers."

—Tracy Steel, speaker, author of *A Redesigned Life*,
and mama of two really cute grumblers

"Motherhood can be hard and beautiful at the same time, filled with moments of wonder and worry, joy and heartache. But if we're not careful, grumbling can fill our hearts and pour out of our mouths in a heartbeat. In her new book *The Grumble-Free Year*, author Tricia Goyer shares her step-by-step journey as she learns to live and teach her children the best way to live a grumble free life. Filled with humbling challenges, teaching moments, and biblical truth, Tricia takes us on an honest and imperfect but ultimately life-changing journey. Developing a heart of thankfulness takes time, so let Tricia share her practical steps and solid Scripture-based concepts that will beautifully guide you as you endeavor to live life grumble free!"

—Kate Battistelli, author of *The God Dare* and *Growing Great Kids*

"Tricia has written a book every family can relate to and learn from in *The Grumble-Free Year*. As well as sharing her family's real-life struggles and successes in their attempt to eliminate grumbling, Tricia offers practical tips and tools for the reader to apply in his or her own home. Most of all, I love the why behind it all—to honor the Lord and find gratitude in the every day. I am leaving this book both encouraged and challenged in a wonderful way!"

—Erin Mohring, cofounder of *Million Praying Moms* and blogger at www.homewiththeboys.net

"Sometimes we just need someone to go first. That's what Tricia and her family did. Now we get to follow in their footsteps and take the challenge ourselves in order to grow an attitude of gratitude in very unique way!"

—Jill Savage, author of *No More Perfect Kids*

"Practicing gratitude is definitely a hallmark of mental health. Tricia Goyer and her family's decision to avoid whining and focus on positivity is a delightful read that can inspire all of us to dwell on a positive approach to life which decreases long-term anxiety and depression and increases lives filled joy and peace."

—Michelle Nietert, MA, LPC-S and clinical director of Community Counseling Associates

"In *The Grumble-Free Year*, Tricia offers us a very real glimpse into her very real family's journey to a more peace-filled and encouraging home. I love that she doesn't give us a ten-step plan but rather shares with us the lessons they learned and the failures they experienced along the way. Full of biblical truth, relatable stories, and practical applications, if you've ever wished for less grumbling in your home, *The Grumble-Free Year* is for you!"

—Teri Lynne Underwood, author of *Praying for Girls*

"I appreciate Goyer's perspective on parenting because she understands the challenges facing families with difficult circumstances, so when she shares her experiences, I lean a little closer and pay attention. She's humbly shown us her journey through a 'grumble-free year,' what worked as well as what didn't, and we can learn as much from her failures as her successes. Several times throughout the book I scrawled 'RELATABLE' in the margins. I started the book thinking, *My crew can't go ONE DAY without grumbling*, and by the end I felt equipped to try. Strap in, kids, we're doing this."

—Melanie Dale, author of *Women Are Scary*,
It's Not Fair, and *Infreakinfertility*

"On the wall of our home is a six-foot wooden sign, 'Thou shalt not whine' We are standing shoulder to shoulder with Tricia, her family, and the thousands of parents and children who want to—and need to—attempt this high calling of a grumble-free year! Philippians 2:14 challenges all to 'do everything without grumbling' and God bless Tricia for showing us all *how*!

—Pam Farrel, bestselling author of *The 10 Best*
Decisions a Parent Can Make and *Men Are*
Like Waffles, Women Are Like Spaghetti

"I need this book. It's all-too-easy to allow complaints and resentments— big and small—to fill my heart, mind, and lips. In *The Grumble-Free Year*, Tricia shares her plan, process, and the gradual results of pursuing a grumble-free existence alongside her family. As you read Tricia's words you'll receive godly wisdom as well as inspiration and motivation to start your own grumble-free path."

    —Katie Orr, creator of the FOCUSed15 Bible Study
       series and author of *Secrets of the Happy Soul*

"In some ways, grumbling is our native language as fallen people. But in *The Grumble-Free Year*, Tricia Goyer helps us learn a different language and a different way of living—and I for one am grateful! Every recovering grumbler needs this book."

    —Joanna Weaver, bestselling author of *Having a Mary Heart in
       a Martha World*, *Having a Mary Spirit*, *Lazarus Awakening*,
       and the award-winning gift book *With This Ring*

The GRUMBLE-FREE Year

The GRUMBLE-FREE Year

Twelve months, eleven family members, and one impossible goal

TRICIA GOYER

NELSON
BOOKS

An Imprint of Thomas Nelson

Published in Nashville, Tennessee, by Nelson Books, an imprint of Thomas Nelson. Nelson Books and Thomas Nelson are registered trademarks of HarperCollins Christian Publishing, Inc.

Published in association with Books & Such Literary Management, 52 Mission Circle, Suite 122, PMB 170, Santa Rosa, California 95409-5370, www.booksandsuch.com.

Thomas Nelson titles may be purchased in bulk for educational, business, fund-raising, or sales promotional use. For information, please e-mail SpecialMarkets@ThomasNelson.com.

ISBN 978-1-4002-1081-7 (eBook)

Library of Congress Cataloging-in-Publication Data

Names: Goyer, Tricia, author.
Title: The grumble-free year : twelve months, eleven family members, and
  one impossible goal / Tricia Goyer.
Description: Nashville : Thomas Nelson, 2019.
Identifiers: LCCN 2019014875 (print) | ISBN 9781400210787 (pbk.)
Subjects: LCSH: Gratitude--Religious aspects--Christianity--Miscellanea.|
  Satisfaction--Religious aspects--Christianity--Miscellanea. |
  Negativism--Miscellanea.
Classification: LCC BV4647.G8 G69 2019 (print) | LCC BV4647.G8 (ebook)|
  DDC 265/.63--dc23
LC record available at https://lccn.loc.gov/2019014875
LC ebook record available at https://lccn.loc.gov/2019980057

Printed in the United States of America

19 20 21 22 23 LSC 10 9 8 7 6 5 4 3 2 1

Dedicated to my husband, kids, and grandma, who dared to take on this impossible grumble-free challenge. What a journey! May this year mold your future. I know it has molded mine.

CONTENTS

CONTENTS

INTRODUCTION

One Sunday night my husband, John, and I talked to our family about the potential challenge of living a grumble-free year. We were finally sitting down for dinner in a restaurant at 10 p.m. after traveling 2,500 miles over the last three days. It was the first time we had all gathered around the table face-to-face in a week. On the other two travel nights, we'd sat scattered around small tables at fast-food restaurants. It was easier pretending our audacious offspring were other people's kids fighting over the fries that had spilled onto the paper-lined tray that way. "Hey, you got three extra fries. Not fair! I'm not going to let you borrow my DVD player for the next two hundred miles!"

Now my stomach clenched, despite the non-deep-fried aromas coming from the restaurant kitchen. My knees quivered under the wooden table (an upgrade from brown Formica). Parenting was hard enough. Did I honestly want to pinky promise the next twelve months of my life to a fleeting fantasy that my children could communicate without complaint and retort without repine?

I softly bit my lip, knowing I had to try—we had to try. Communication in our home had dropped to the level of mumbles and grumbles, moans and whines. We couldn't live this way anymore—unless I invested in noise-canceling headphones. The problem was, society frowned upon parents who muted their children. More importantly, even if I couldn't hear the rumbles, it wouldn't mean my children weren't bemoaning Every. Single. Thing. In. Their. Lives.

"I've been talking with my agent about writing a book that involves all of you." My lips pressed into a tight smile. "But maybe this isn't the best time to discuss it since it's so late and we've just driven so far." (As I calculated, we'd gone the equivalent to the distance between Barcelona, Spain, and Moscow, Russia, taking all the back roads.)

"Mom, you have to tell us now," pleaded fourteen-year-old Maddie as she sat next to her twin, Grace, who bounced in her seat. These two were the most active of our bunch of eight traveling children. They laughed loud, lived big, and made the Tasmanian devil look like an innocent, frolicking lamb in comparison.

"Will the book include our names and pictures?" asked twelve-year-old Alexis. "Will we become famous?" Fame was very important to Alexis, who would tell every new person she met that her mom had walked the red carpet. (Yes, I did walk the red carpet at Grauman's Chinese Theatre after I wrote the novelization of the movie *Moms' Night Out*.) Having been moved around quite a bit in foster care since she was five years old, Alexis had learned how to make friends quickly. I could see from the twinkle in her eyes that any chance to be "known" and become popular she would consider a win.

"I don't know about pictures, but I will use your names. Or at least pseudonyms," I answered.

Grace stopped her bouncing. "What's that?" she called too

loudly. Thankfully there were very few other customers that time of night.

"They're false names." John stirred his straw in his soda. "It's just safer that way."

I nodded. "That's right. You might not want everyone reading this book to google you."

"I want everyone googling me." Alexis smiled and tossed her dark hair back over her shoulder. "Because I'm fabulous."

I chuckled. "Yes, yes, I know you are."

"I don't want everyone to google me. That's creepy." Grace looked to her twin to back her up. When Maddie nodded in agreement, Grace's eyes glanced back and focused on mine. "What's my name going to be? I get to help pick it, right?"

"Of course. If we decide we want to do this challenge." I chuckled at her enthusiasm as I shook my head and gave in to the kids' demands to keep talking. "We can talk about it. We don't have to start right away. It's just something we have to think about."

A chorus of voices rose in unison. "What is it?"

I looked to John. He nodded, urging me on.

"Well, our idea is called *A Grumble-Free Year: A Family of Eleven Takes on the Challenge*, or something like that."

Grace's eyes widened. "Haha, you're funny."

Maddie shook her head. "Yeah, right."

"I think we can do it!" piped up seven-year-old Aly. I looked down at her as she sat serenely next to me. She gave me her puppy-dog-eye look, feigning innocence. As if.

"I think we can too," added nine-year-old Sissy. Those two were usually quieter, and their eagerness to take on the challenge surprised me.

"Wait, what are we doing?" six-year-old Buddy asked. The

youngest boy after six girls in a row, he was used to conversations swirling around him. Lots of chattery, dramatic conversation, and it usually took him a minute to catch on.

Voices rose, with those who believed in the project speaking up and others who thought the idea was crazy adding their thoughts to the mix.

I projected my voice over the din. "We know it sounds challenging. Dad and I know it'll take a lot of work, and that's why we want to offer an incentive." I turned to John. "Do you want to tell them?"

"Okay. Like Mom said, we've been talking about it, and this is going to take a lot of intention from all of us and a lot of working together. But if we try really hard, I was thinking we could all go on a cruise at the end of the year—to celebrate a year of working to be grumble-free."

Excitement built with questions about the cruise. My favorite was from Grace: "Can we have our own beds on the ship?" When you come from a large family that likes to travel, the question made sense. We usually piled kids into beds in hotel rooms or sometimes on the floor.

I laughed. "Yes, I'm sure we'll find a way for everyone to have his or her own bed."

"Wait!" Alexis lifted two hands in the air, trying to get our attention. "Does this mean we're going to have a famous writer with us, following us around twenty-four hours a day?"

I lifted one eyebrow and narrowed my gaze at her. "Uh, I am a writer who lives with you and follows you around twenty-four hours a day."

Laughter filled the air.

Alexis shrank down into her seat. "Oh, yeah. I forgot."

"What about you, Anna?" I turned to our seventeen-year-old daughter, who hadn't made a peep yet. She was the easygoing one of the bunch who didn't get her feathers ruffled often. Also, she was one of the ones I would rarely hear complain.

"I think we have a fifty-fifty chance of succeeding," she commented. "With this group, I think it'll be hard."

I looked to twenty-three-year-old Nathan next. He was our youngest biological child, and he had gone from being the youngest to having seven younger siblings. Like Anna, he was a contemplative soul who rarely complained, but he was our child who'd been most impacted by the adoptions as we went from a quiet house to one filled with disruption. Numerous times every day, when whines and moans followed every request from me, Nathan would look at me with his Eeyore-like gaze, as if saying, "Can't we do something about all this complaining and whining, Mom?"

I'd try, of course, to get them to stop. "No need to complain about that," I'd say. Or, "Let's try to say that again without whining." My favorite was, "I don't understand Whine-ese. Why don't you try again?" But my constant reminders did nothing to bring about change.

Nathan crossed his arms, set them on the table, and nodded. "I won't say it's impossible, but . . ."

"But?" I asked.

He lifted his eyebrows and sighed, as if truly understanding the difficulty of the challenge. "Like Anna said, it'll be hard, but it's worth a shot."

"That's the important thing to remember—this is going to be hard," John responded. "It's not as if we're trying to be perfect. Instead, it's something we'll need to work on."

"But does this mean we can't tell people when we need something?" Alexis asked. "Will we have to be good all the time?"

As we waited for our food, John explained a bit more. "No one's good all the time. Even Mom and I mess up . . . a lot. God doesn't expect any of us to be perfect, but complaining is something he takes seriously. Remember how Moses led the Israelites into the desert according to God's command? Well, they had a lot of needs in that desert, and God knew that. But instead of asking God to meet their needs—and trusting he would—the Israelites complained. Complaining is wanting our way without treating others—or God—with respect."

Everyone listened, and I was surprised how well they were paying attention, although I shouldn't have been. Each time we'd added children to our home through adoption, we had experienced a lot of challenges, yet John and I had learned that the kids' wrong behavior mostly came from not being taught what was right. Time and time again when we taught right behavior and attitudes, the kids rose to the occasion. We had already taught our kids big things, like how to talk rather than yell and how to keep our personal spaces neat and clean (well, we were still working on that). We taught chores and how to support each other within our home. Now it was time to train our kids on the little habits that sometimes were easy to overlook—things that nibbled away at the peace and joy in our home, bit by bit. Things like grumbling.

From the conversation around the restaurant table, it sounded like everyone was on board, and I took a deep breath. The weariness of the trip intensified as the responsibility of what the year to come now held rushed over me. Suddenly the idea became reality, and the project became serious. I knew, because we'd mentioned both the challenge and the cruise, the kids would never let us back down now. Never.

I also knew this challenge had to start with John and me. We needed to set up a framework that would teach and guide our kids without discouraging them. Setting basic goals for ourselves would be the first place to start.

I sighed as the waitress approached our table with the first tray of food. I took the cloth napkin from the table and spread it across my lap, both worry and excitement causing my stomach to do a small flip. This challenge was going to be harder for me than I thought, but it would also be so worth it. Taking a family of eleven, full of personalities and viewpoints and individual struggles, through an entire year without grumbling was a monumental task, but I sensed we were on the verge of something special. And I couldn't wait to see what God had in the works.

Part 1

GEARING UP

Chapter 1

PERFECTLY IMPERFECT

I grew up as a perfect child in an imperfect home, or at least that's how it seemed to me. My mom was a single mom, and we lived with my grandparents for the first four years of my life. I didn't know my biological dad—he wasn't in the picture—but for my early years it didn't seem to matter. As the oldest child and grandchild, my mom, two aunts, and grandparents doted on me. I'm sure, like everyone else, I believed I could do no wrong.

My mom married my stepdad when I was four years old, and I was an easy bonus to have around. When my brother joined our family, we took on two unique roles. Me: perfect older sister. Him: terrorizing younger brother. In our little family of four, I was the one who obeyed, got good grades, and rarely grumbled. Well, at least not too loudly.

But even with my brother being that terrorizing younger sibling, there wasn't a lot of yelling or obvious whining in our home. My family members held their emotions close. Complaints were voiced under one's breath. When other families went on vacation, my parents or grandparents might mumble something like, "Must be nice." Other common phrases were, "Gee, wish I could get some help here," or "What am I . . . everyone's slave?" There were few demands or big displays of disapproval, but there was grumbling. Under-the-breath grumbling was how we showed our disapproval with others or with life.

Once, a family member did blow up at a family holiday. His voice rose to loud shouts, and everyone in the room froze. In anger, he stormed out of the house and was gone for hours. When he left, no one said a word about what had happened. We just went on enjoying our holiday meal as if there wasn't tension in the air. Even worse, no one said a word to him after he returned. Big emotions scared us, and I learned the only safe way to share emotions was through quiet grumbling.

⋇

Marriage is amazing in how it brings together two unique people with different backgrounds and various ways of handling issues and conflict. I grew up learning how to be good, to avoid conflict, and not to yell (but grumble instead). And then I got married, and amazingly John wasn't raised in the same type of home I was.

When John was growing up, his family handled things differently. His parents were strong Christians, and when John was in high school his dad became a pastor. John's parents were firm but kind. They set the rules and the kids followed. His parents, like mine, also struggled financially. His father changed jobs quite a lot, and they moved often. Even though they had little, John's family found ways to be thankful about what they had and what God was doing.

As John and I prepared to embark on this new journey toward

a grumble-free year, it made sense to look back at where we'd both come from first in order to understand where we would be going together—and how we'd lead our children there.

"I don't remember my parents grumbling about the state of their lives," my husband told me as we sat down to discuss this challenge. "Sure, they wished they had more and better things, but they didn't grumble about it. And when I got older, I did what I could to help them. I bought my own clothes. And when I got an after-school job at a grocery store, I'd even buy groceries for them."

As I listened to John, I made a mental note. *Help kids see they can help out more instead of grumbling about what they don't have.* The idea of such a thing seemed like a pipe dream, but as I looked back at our marriage it seemed as if God had been preparing John and me for this very thing: to teach our kids how to communicate well and not fall back into the destructive, grumbling pattern that I found myself in—a pattern that could have seriously damaged our marriage.

⚬

When John and I first got married, there was little conflict. Partly because John is naturally a content person, but also because by then I'd learned to hold most of my grumbles inside, one step further than the quiet, under-my-breath grumbling I'd been raised with.

After I dedicated my life to God at age seventeen, I knew that having a joyful spirit was part of the Christian life. Not that I was perfect. There were seasons when I wasn't. At only twenty-three years old I had three small kids at home, and it was both overwhelming and tiring, especially when they grew old enough to start complaining and grumbling themselves.

As we were raising our three oldest kids, our parenting style was "Let's talk about this." Whenever we heard one of our three kids grumbling, we'd sit down with them. We'd talk about what they were thinking and feeling, and we'd try to get them to see a different perspective. If we heard grumbles about something their friends were allowed to do, we'd explain why it wasn't a good idea for our family—why we had different rules and choices. And of course we tried to model keeping our own grumbles at bay.

The thing is, though, my attempts to model what I thought to be correct behavior easily led me back into certain mindsets from my childhood that were not healthy. So while we employed a "Let's talk about this" method with our kids, I unconsciously began doing the opposite thing myself. There were problems and issues that needed to be worked through, but instead of talking to others about them, I held them all inside, not wanting to complain.

To me, grumbling was something negative I just needed to deal with. Holding grumbles inside didn't hurt others . . . well, not really. Not until my inward grumbles created a wedge in my marriage.

⁂

By the time I'd been married for fifteen years, from the looks of things we had the perfect life, the perfect marriage, the nearly perfect kids. A homeschooling mom of three, I had just started to get books published and had helped launch a crisis pregnancy center. We lived in a nice house, drove nice cars, served in church, and rarely ever grumbled.

Yet, even while on the outside it seemed everything was going great, inside I felt both overwhelmed and empty. As a woman of God, I poured myself out continually to my family, church, and community. I did all the cooking, most of the shopping, homeschooled, volunteered often, and wrote books. Soon the old habits I'd learned growing up emerged.

When someone got a weekend away: "Must be nice."

When my kids didn't do their chores when and how I wanted them to: "Who do they think I am, their slave?"

When my husband spent the evening talking or watching a movie with friends: "It's not fair. I'd like to just be able to sit for five minutes."

I wasn't angry—at least I didn't think I was—but the grumbling confirmed the story in my head: *I do everything for everybody, and no one does anything for me.* It was a lie, of course, but my unsettled discontent told me it was truth. And then, out of the blue, an old boyfriend emailed, inquiring about my life. As I told him about our family, my work, and my volunteering, he confirmed what my grumbling mind had repeated over and over again: no one truly appreciates you. Of course he had a motive for his assessment. *I'd be different. I'd appreciate you, just like I used to when we were dating.*

Even though I knew it wasn't a good idea, I gave my old boyfriend my phone number, and he called one afternoon just to chat.

"You do so much." His voice was filled with compassion. "It sounds like your family takes advantage of you. I bet they don't even thank you for all you do. I wouldn't let you work so hard . . ." His slick words confirmed what I'd been feeling deep inside. He gave voice to my inner grumbles.

I'm not appreciated.
I do everything for everybody.
If my family really loved me, they'd see my needs.
Maybe there is someone out there who would really see me, who'd be thankful for all I do.

My mind repeated those thoughts as I went through the next few days taking care of everyone. And even though my life hadn't changed on the outside, inside the grumbles transformed into a huge burden, weighing me down.

Instead of drawing near to my husband and kids, I felt a wedge coming between us. More than anything I wanted to talk to my old boyfriend again—to hear his words about how wonderful I was—and that scared me. I'd had friends who had been drawn away from their marriages by smooth words and caring actions from another person. I had no doubt that if I spoke with my old boyfriend again it would lead to no good. His words had shifted my heart and mind away from everything good to only focus on everything wrong. It scared me that such simple flattery could turn my heart so swiftly, and I knew this couldn't go on.

Knowing the communication was wrong, I confessed to my husband that I'd been talking with my old boyfriend, then I broke it off. It wasn't easy—the confession or breaking off communication. It hurt John deeply that I'd even make a connection again with someone from my past. I also realized how vulnerable I'd allowed myself to become. Why? Because I'd had unreasonable and unmet expectations—expectations of receiving help even when I didn't ask for it. Expectations of having everyone thank me for my contributions to my family, even though I didn't offer thanks to others often enough.

As Adele Ahberg Calhoun said, "Unmet expectations are resentments and disappointments waiting to happen,"[1] and as my inner grumbles grew, so did the resentment in my heart.

By expecting my husband, kids, and even friends to automatically know what I wanted and needed, I felt empty, exhausted, and unfulfilled. So when someone I'd once "loved" offered to swoop in and fill those needs, it was a tempting offer. It also showed me that my heart, mind, and attitude needed a lot of work.

From this experience, I learned not to hold everything inside. I shared, through tears, what had drawn me to my old boyfriend: appreciation. And I poured out all the ways I'd felt unappreciated around our home—not only for months, but for years.

My husband's jaw dropped at my words, and tears filled his eyes too. "I didn't have any idea all those feelings were inside you," he confessed.

Of course he hadn't. In my effort not to grumble, I hadn't voiced my needs. I'd been foolish to expect my husband to meet my needs when I hadn't even expressed what they were.

I soon started expressing things I needed to my husband and my kids: time away, date nights, more help around the house—and surprisingly, amazingly, my family responded.

Even though I didn't fully understand it at the time, this was the beginning of my own grumble-free journey. It was a journey of highs and lows. It was also a foundation for what was to come. Because of this, later, as our family started on our grumble-free journey together, I thought it would be more about helping my kids than anything else. I didn't fully understand how much more work God still wanted to do in my life. After all, I'd already been on my own journey and thought I was doing well. But it turns out, the work he'd started years ago was simply building the groundwork for all he wanted to do now. I may have thought the Grumble-Free Year would be mostly about "them," my family, when we first started, but, as you will see within these pages, every change I wanted to see in them ended up having to be worked out in me first.

Reflection Questions

1. How was grumbling handled during your growing-up years?
2. What grumbling habits did you carry into adulthood?
3. How has grumbling (outward or inward) impacted your life?
4. What do you think would be harder: trying to tackle your own grumbling or attempting to help others do the same?

Your Turn

Take a few minutes and consider your growing-up years. How did your family deal with disappointment? Did they communicate well? Did they attempt to focus on speaking with thankfulness and gratitude, even during challenging circumstances?

Maybe, like me, you only wished that was the case. Find a piece of paper and jot down how your family acted: With anger or rage? With passive disapproval and grumbling? Next, consider what habits you brought into your current home—both for the good and the bad. If possible, ask your spouse to do the same.

Also, while for most of the book I will share how we worked toward not grumbling out loud as a family, it's important to note that it's not good to hold all our grumbling inside either. Good communication is sharing what's really going on inside our hearts. It's not okay to hold in all our frustrations and disappointments for the sake of not grumbling.

If sharing what's really going on in your heart with your family is something you need to work on, then start with that first. Ask

God to help you share truth with others, even when it's hard. Also learn to listen as others do the same.

Truly succeeding at this challenge means communicating well with our families and having the gratitude we hold deep inside make its way to our lips time and time again.

Chapter 2

ME FIRST

So how's everything going?" my husband, John, inquired as I was making dinner. His hands reached up and squeezed my shoulders. I winced at first, then I felt myself relax as he started to rub them.

"Honestly?" I asked as I added the onion to the hamburger I was browning.

"Honestly." He paused the massage and leaned against the kitchen counter so he could look into my eyes.

"Well, I'm nervous about the book I turned in last week. I haven't heard anything from my editor yet. And homeschool today wasn't the best. I lost my temper again. And my feet hurt. I've been doing laundry, and I don't think I've sat most of the afternoon."

John nodded. "How about I take the kids for a walk after dinner—to give you a bit of quiet?"

A soft smile touched my lips. "Thank you. That would be great."

Commotion sounded from the backyard, and John moved in that direction to investigate. As he did, I bit my lip. *Was I just grumbling?* I replayed the conversation, worried that I was. But as the meat sizzled in the pan, I told myself to relax. John had asked how things were going. And even if he hadn't, it was okay to tell my husband my worries, the day's challenges, and my needs. It was something I'd learned—and was still in the process of learning.

Overcoming my internal grumbles, transforming my thoughts and attitude, and talking about my needs—and having them met by the people I loved—had transformed my marriage and my relationship with my kids. My heart had opened up to my family as I realized I could actually share a problem or something that was bothering me and my family would listen. I didn't have to keep my needs to myself. Instead of internally grumbling, I could be honest and transparent . . . well, at least most of the time.

Even though more than a dozen years had passed since I'd decided to communicate better about what was really going on in my heart, I still felt guilty at times. How I wished I could have smiled and told John, "I had a perfect day. How about you?" But that wouldn't have been the truth. Trying to keep everything inside doesn't help anyone, although the challenge of being able to share what was going on in a truthful way without grumbling had become a thin line, especially as we had added to our family.

Just as our three biological kids were launching into the world, John and I had felt drawn to adoption. In the course of six years we finalized the adoption of seven kids, six of them from foster care, each with their own histories, hurts, and needs. Even though God placed the desire to adopt on our hearts, and even though we were giving children forever homes, it was one of the hardest periods of our lives. Anger, drama, fits, and hurt feelings happened on a daily basis as the kids struggled with the neglect and trauma from their pasts. John and I also struggled with losing every form of comfort, control, and cleanliness we'd previously known.

Overrun with emotional kids, clutter, and laundry, I soon found myself falling into old habits. My needs multiplied as I ran nonstop to meet the needs of everyone in our home. And not wanting any of these kids to feel unwanted or a burden, my mode of expression returned to grumbles—many voiced but even more piling up inside, stacking one upon another, building a wall around my heart and stopping the few good emotions from breaking through. I had no joy. I had no order. I had no peace. Every day I woke up with dread. It would be another day where I had no control and no hope of gaining it. It was a recipe for disaster.

I was at an all-time high for grumbles.

"Whose shoes/socks/toys are these?"
"This place is a mess."
"Why in the world isn't anyone picking up after themselves?"
"Why are you talking to your sister that way?"
"Why are you talking to me that way?"
"Can we just stop with all the yelling?"
"If you grumble one more time . . ."

I needed to spend time bonding and connecting with these kids, but deep down there was an unsettled frustration. I clearly remember one day leaning into a hot van and picking gum up from the carpet with my fingernail.

God, is this really what you called me to? I used to have hours a day to write in my quiet office. Now I not only no longer had a quiet office (my office was moved to my bedroom to make space for more kids), I was spending hours a day cleaning up messes that I knew would be there again tomorrow.

Knowing I needed help, I turned during that time to my friend and life coach Alice. Alice had been my life coach since 2009, and she'd helped me move through a lot of life changes. She was the one who'd first taught me the "how" behind talking to my husband and my kids about my needs instead of carrying all those internal grumbles inside and letting them build.

"So what's going on?" Alice asked when I called her. With that one question everything poured out.

"I know God called us to these kids, but I don't know how I can do it. I feel as if I've lost control of my life. I don't feel capable of taking care of all their needs. There are so many messes and so much clutter. Our space hasn't grown any bigger, but we've added seven more people to it. I can't even walk from the front door to the kitchen without stepping over eleven pairs of shoes, and no one listens to me as I try to find some sense of order."

"It sounds like there are a lot of negative thoughts going on in your mind," Alice commented. "Let's see if we can work on that."

I sucked in a breath and furrowed my brow. *My thoughts. Are my thoughts really the problem? That can't be it. These children's messes and my lack of control are the real problems, right?*

Still, I was willing to try anything.

One of the first activities Alice had me do was to get a piece of paper and on one side—in black ink—list everything I believed was wrong at this time.

I offered a sarcastic huff. "I might need two pieces of paper."

"Well, if it takes two pieces of paper, that's fine too." I could hear the smile in Alice's words over the phone.

And then I began my list:

- My house is always a mess.
- The laundry is never-ending.

- My work and writing are getting behind as I focus on the kids.
- The kids seem to always be angry and fighting.
- Nothing seems to be right. They grumble constantly.

I wrote about a dozen more things, then Alice asked me to read the list to her.

"Wow, that's a lot," she said in a compassionate tone. "I can see these things are really bothering you. They would bother me too. I can see why you feel stressed and why you find yourself grumbling all the time . . . even if most of it is in your mind."

Then Alice gave me a new assignment. She wanted me to write a positive statement to offset each negative one, writing these statements in blue ink. "The statement has to be proactive, what you're going to do about it. For example, for 'My house is always a mess,' you can write, 'My children are capable of helping me clean the house.'"

Just hearing those words kicked my mind into gear. I immediately thought of the chore chart I'd started to create but never finished. I also thought about my kids asking for allowances. John and I had put off setting that up, but perhaps we could combine the two.

Alice went on to explain the importance of focusing on the opposite of our current struggles. The opposite of weakness is strength. The opposite of helplessness is efficiency. The opposite of anxiety is paying attention to what is right and what is possible. Our thoughts are just thoughts, not facts. They're just a story we're telling ourselves.

It took me a minute to process that. My grumbles were just a story—a negative story—about how my life was working at the moment. In an effort to survive, my mind was pointing out all the "dangers" of this new life. My mind was attempting to keep me safe, but I didn't have to make the negative story my story. The thing was, it would take a conscious effort to choose differently, just like it had taken conscious efforts to let my husband know my needs over the years.

"Life is going to throw problems at you all the time," Alice said. "We have a choice every single time of how we're going to respond. So do you understand your homework for the week?"

"Yes, I'm going through this list and coming up with proactive ways to deal with these problems."

"Wonderful. That's how this works. Your mind knows there's a problem, and if you're not taking responsibility for that problem, your mind feels as if you're in danger. I'm eager to see what will happen when your mind switches and you start coming up with solutions to these problems."

I thanked Alice and hung up the phone. Then I looked over my list, eager to come up with proactive statements—ones that would give my mind new tracks to run on. Ones that would give me solutions to focus on instead of remaining stuck in negative ruts.

- My house is always a mess. ⇒ My children are capable of helping me clean the house.
- The laundry is never-ending. ⇒ We can come up with an effective laundry solution.
- My work and writing are getting behind as I focus on the kids. ⇒ I can come up with doable work hours, even if it means hiring help.
- The kids seem to always be angry and fighting. ⇒ We are working to find healing through therapy, and I can work

with the therapists to teach my kids appropriate interactions and reactions.

- Nothing seems to be right. They grumble constantly. ⇒ We can work toward becoming grumble-free.

Out of all of these problems, I began working on solutions to the more tangible ones first. I finished setting up the chore chart, and I hired my twenty-three-year-old son to watch the children a couple of hours in the afternoons so I could work. Our therapists assisted me in coming up with plans for helping my children deal with anger and fighting. These were all good steps I was taking in the right direction, and I was thankful to have reset my thinking about them. And yet that last one about grumbling still seemed elusive, and I struggled to move beyond the doubts that kept creeping back into my mind.

I suppose there are just some things I need to learn to deal with, I told myself. *After all, what else should I expect after adding seven children to our home in such a short amount of time?*

Maybe grumbling is just something I need to learn to accept.

That's where my mind hovered for years.

There's only so much we can do, I told myself. With that many kids, who'd ever be able to tackle such a big, elusive problem like grumbling?

And then, for some crazy reason, God brought the idea of the Grumble-Free Year into our lives. It had been a while since that conversation with Alice, and I definitely still struggled with seeing how we could possibly begin to cut grumbling out of our daily existence. But even as I finished making dinner, I realized there had been one big change over the years. Instead of seeing grumbling as a small issue we were going to have to live with, I'd now fixed it in my mind that it was something we all really could work on. We would just need some serious help from God to see how to begin.

Reflection Questions

1. In what ways do you find yourself overwhelmed with the negative things in your life?
2. How would the story you're telling yourself change if you started focusing on solutions instead of problems?
3. Has grumbling been something you've previously believed cannot be changed? What could happen if you put some intention behind having a grumble-free year?

Your Turn

What negative thoughts are weighing you down? Which ones are especially sinking in and creating ruts in your mind as you circle around them again and again?

Get a piece of paper and draw one line down the middle, from top to bottom. On the left side write down everything that's wrong about your life right now. What problems do you seem to be stuck on? What's not working in this season of your life?

When you're finished, write down solutions for those problems. Kick your brain out of the "caution, caution, caution" mode into finding solutions. For each problem, turn it around and state a proactive solution.

Everything doesn't need to be fixed overnight, but set your

mind to work on solutions instead of struggles. And next time those warning signals pop up, tell yourself, "Yes, I already know—and we're working on a solution for that." Remind yourself that meditating on the problems and grumbling about them doesn't help, but focusing on finding fixes does.

Chapter 3

IT'S TIME TO THRIVE, NOT JUST SURVIVE, AS A FAMILY

T he day was not off to a great start.

My husband was back in town after being away for work, which I was thankful for, but with him home I'd finally been able to slow down enough to look around and realize our place was a mess. I suppose eleven people living in one house will do that.

Currently in our home were John and me, my eighty-eight-year-old grandmother, and eight of our ten kids ages twenty-three, seventeen, fourteen, fourteen, twelve, nine, seven, and six. The oldest and youngest of the kids at home were boys, and the rest were girls. Our daughter Leslie lived in Europe with her husband, but our son Cory and his two kids lived nearby. We also had a few other young families we unofficially called ours, so in the course of a day, there could be between eleven and twenty people in our home. That's a lot of people to care for and feed. I didn't mind the cooking, but the messes got to me.

John had taken the kids grocery shopping, which was my cue to clean out the fridge to make room. So I found myself gingerly picking through leftovers that hadn't gotten eaten and wiping up caked-on spills no one had bothered to clean up. Then I moved to the pantry. *Oh yuck.* I'd been ignoring the pantry for a while. Spilled cereal, something brown and sticky all over the cans, three jars of open peanut butter with smears all over the outside.

The grumbling that had started in my mind soon spilled out of my mouth, oozing and stinking just like the gunk I'd scrubbed off the glass refrigerator shelves. "This is ridiculous. My kids are slobs. Why do I get left with this mess?"

By the time John returned with groceries—way more groceries than I thought we needed—my mood had soured. My family walked in giggling, laughing, and plopping grocery bags around the kitchen with abandon, like food fairies and a jolly elf populating a food desert. For the last hour they'd been dancing around the cereal aisles and produce section while I'd been chiseling cemented syrup off pantry shelves.

As they started to put things away, they obviously didn't notice that half the shelves were still littered with stale rice cereal, fossilized raisins, and dust because my husband and kids proceeded to blithely pull cans and boxes out of grocery bags and skip their way to the pantry, shoving everything in. I stood in the middle of the kitchen, cleaning cloth hanging limp in my hand. My family members flowed around me, a boulder in their path.

As I stood there, six-year-old Buddy approached me. His white-blond hair was buzzed in a military haircut, and the summer sun had already given him a light golden tan. "Look, Mommy. Daddy bought us fruit snacks!" His smile carried all the way up to his baby-blue eyes.

Next to him, nine-year-old Sissy bounced as she pushed her glasses up on her nose. "And we got ice cream and root beer. Daddy says after we clean our rooms we can make root beer floats!"

I nodded, acknowledging their words, but my attention wasn't fully on them. Instead, it was on the teens carrying armfuls of cans to the pantry. Inwardly I groaned, knowing that if they continued to put stuff away, things would be even harder to clean.

"I'm not done cleaning out the pantry yet. Don't put anything away until I'm done!" My voice boomed like a clap of thunder from a dark storm cloud.

The lilting voices stopped. Half a dozen sets of eyes turned in my direction. Buddy took a step back, and a scowl filled his face.

John glanced over, eyebrows lifted in surprise, as if seeing me for the first time.

I lifted my dirty rag and rolled my eyes. Somebody had been doing the dirty work around here, and they hadn't even noticed. "The pantry is disgusting, and shoving in more stuff doesn't help," I spouted.

My family's previously curved-up smiles now drooped, wilted and limp.

John's gaze narrowed slightly. He opened his mouth as if wanting to scold me, but then he thought better of it. "C'mon, kids. Mom wants to tackle this alone."

So they all left, filing out of the kitchen like six of the dwarfs leaving me, Grumpy, behind. I glanced at the grocery bags and contents spilled onto the countertops. The quietness, where there'd been laughter a minute before, mocked me.

"Well, that showed them," I grumbled to myself. *Now you really have a mess to clean up,* my mind chided. And it wasn't just the grocery mess.

With a heavy heart and lots of frustrating thoughts filling my mind, I grabbed the cleaner and moved back to the pantry with my rag. The mental grumbling didn't stop until the Holy Spirit started trying to insert some comments. *You should apologize,* and *They were just trying to help.*

I knew Mr. H. S. was right. He's the voice of God, after all. The grumbles had started with the first swipe of my wet rag over the dirty fridge shelf and then had taken over my day. It wasn't until after I'd already exploded, griping at my family, that I remembered about our commitment to the Grumble-Free Year.

We hadn't quite begun in earnest yet, but I had already made a list of activities we'd be doing over the next few months. They all sounded great on paper, but the problem was reality. The reality that this attempt was happening in the middle of real life with eleven very sinful people, me at the top of the list!

I think that's what worried me most about the project. How was I going to lead and motivate my family when I still had some serious work to do on this issue? Sure, it was great to think ahead, to talk to a life coach, to understand the negative tracks our minds get on, and to try to be proactive about making positive changes. But then real life hits, with real emotions, and everything crumbles from there.

※

Even though I understood how to take control of negative thoughts, there were still those times when they looped in my mind and grumbles sprouted up—a lot. Reality hit me hard as I was forced to face all the ways I so often failed in this area and to acknowledge that I needed God to help me form a more realistic plan for me and my family to confront this weakness in our lives.

After I finished cleaning the kitchen, I returned to the list I'd created with a newly humbled heart. I needed to remind myself often why I was doing this. Otherwise, none of the "hows" I had thought of would gain traction.

What were my goals for a grumble-free year? I jotted them down:

- I want to foster meaningful relationships within our family. Grumbling puts wedges between people. Grumbling about others brings strife.
- I want our kids to be caring and compassionate adults. Grumbling is thinking of ourselves instead of others. The only way we can grow compassion is to replace the grumbling in our hearts with gratitude and care for others.
- I want my kids to be hardworking and responsible. I want them to learn that there will be tough stuff in life but grumbling about these things won't solve problems.
- I want to change. I want to be a role model. I want to catch myself complaining and become a child of God who will inspire others for good.

After looking over my list, I knew what I needed to do first. I sought out my family, starting with my husband and then going to each of my kids. "I'm sorry about my attitude. I know you were just trying to help. All the mess bothered me, and I let the grumbles take over. Will you forgive me?"

One by one my family responded with the same answer: "Yes." And not surprisingly, they also offered hugs. Maybe we could do this after all.

Change must always start with our hearts. As I thought about the Grumble-Free Year, it was obvious it had to start in my heart. And it had to start in my kids' hearts too.

Grumbling is something we do by default. As Alice had told me earlier, focusing on the negative is the mind's effort to watch out for danger—and it's a muddy rut we can get stuck in. So unless we're intentional about uprooting this in our hearts, it'll tend to stay put and keep growing. The hard thing is that grumbling is not only something we naturally lean toward, but the world is excellent at teaching this habit as well. Everywhere we look there are messages about needing more or better things.

When the neighbor gets a new bike: "Mom, my bike's old and falling apart."

When an American Girl catalog arrives in the mail: "Why do I have to wait until my birthday? I want this now. It's not fair."

When my teens are hanging out with others at youth group: "I'm the only one without a cell phone/TV in my room [and a dozen other things we don't let them have]. It's so lame."

Worse are messages that my kids themselves aren't enough— not beautiful enough, smart enough, talented enough, cool enough. Once, when noticing my teen daughter was in a funk, I asked her about it.

"Every time I look in the mirror, I see everything wrong with me. I can't see anything right."

Oh, honey, I wanted to tell her. *I understand.*

Even for me, everywhere I look there are tips on how to lose ten pounds, have fewer wrinkles, and have more luscious hair. Why can't I be thinner, younger looking, and have a flowing, glowing mane?

Then there was the issue of trying to do it all: have an amazing career, volunteer for great causes, and raise God-honoring children, all while tending a perfectly designed house and cooking healthy dinners. What happens when that's not possible? We gripe about it—to ourselves, to others. And no one really seems to notice our discontent or expect anything different. They even applaud our unhappiness and dissatisfaction as we "keep it real." Everyone grumbles, right?

We also grumble when we can't find a good parking place or the right size of the cute shirt on sale. The weather, the traffic, our child's homework, our work that we bring home. We complain about the price of things, the vacations we wish we were taking, and politics. Always politics.

And while it seems everyone's doing it, doesn't it also seem that everyone's doing it more? I'd go into more detail about all the grumbling I've heard in just the last week, but I'm worried that might seem like grumbling—and I don't want to fill this book with what I'm trying to avoid.

So where does all this grumbling come from?

GRUMBLE: verb
1580 from Middle French *grommeler* "mutter between the teeth" or directly from Middle Dutch *grommelen* "murmur, mutter, grunt," from *grommen* "to rumble, growl." Imitative, or perhaps akin to *grim*. Related: grumbled; grumbling.

Grumbling is taking a grim look at ourselves and the world around us and muttering about it between our teeth. It is an easy habit to start but a hard one to break.

As I think back on my grumbling attitude that first day in the kitchen, I realize maybe part of my grumbling came from my desire to feel powerful while truly feeling powerless. Anger feels powerful, and playing a victim often causes others to jump to action. When I play the victim, I deny others the joyful and peaceful attitude they want from me in an effort to get them to do what I want, and this is a bad trap not just for me but also for my kids to fall into. After all, do I want them to think this is how one gets what he or she wants, by becoming a victim? And do I want them to learn to please and pacify those who see themselves as victims just to bring peace? What a horrible way to live.

I knew, as we looked to start the journey for the year, that we had the grumbling down pat. Yes, that muttering between the teeth was pretty common around here. And as I looked around, I saw that all this grumbling had allowed us to disown any responsibility. Since things couldn't be perfect, we didn't take ownership for our choices, attitudes, or actions. By grumbling we showed our disapproval, but we also made it clear we believed we had no ability to change things, whether our words, beliefs, or behaviors.

So maybe, as part of the first step of starting with our hearts, we needed to develop a better view of life—a hopeful one, not a grim one. Maybe when we sealed our lips to grumbling, we'd instead discover ways to make changes and find our power. These changes could be external, like teaching our children to do a better job at taking care of our pantry. Or they could be more internal, such as unsubscribing from magazines or catalogs that caused underlying feelings of discontent. Changes could be made, but it would take refusing to put our energy into simply grumbling about them and instead actually doing something—and not just anything, but working to make disciples rather than simply punishing our kids for grumbling.

"Too often we forget that discipline really means to teach, not to punish," wrote Daniel J. Siegel and Tina Payne Bryson in their book *The Whole-Brain Child*. "A disciple is a student, not a recipient of behavioral consequences."[1]

And that's something else I understood now too—how unfair I'd been. I'd been quick to get on my children about grumbling while at the same time I hadn't worked at teaching them what to do instead. While the kids were eager to get started on our project, truthfully, I'd been putting it off. I mean, you can't fail what you don't start, right? But I couldn't continue living in this paralyzing fear of the big job in front of us. Maybe it was time to remind myself of all we had come through and all God was calling us into.

-ϙ́-

When John and I started adopting children, we had one goal: simply survive. In 2013, we added two special-needs children to our home, and, looking back, I can see that my grumbling rose then due to my own feelings of powerlessness. I didn't know how to handle all their issues at once. Even though I knew we were called to adopt, I became overwhelmed by caring for their needs. My life no longer looked like my life, and grumbling became my go-to when I felt unsure how to bring about changes.

At two and a half years old, Buddy was barely talking and he showed all the symptoms for RAD (Reactive Attachment Disorder). He didn't connect with us, his caregivers, but instead would go to anyone to have his needs met. He was especially drawn to older, scruffy men. I can't count the number of times he'd run away from me in the grocery store and grasped the leg of someone who looked dirty and downright scary. One of the things I worked hardest on was training Buddy to come to me for help, for answers, for love.

Buddy was evaluated and found to be in need of physical, occupational, and speech therapy, but discovering his needs and seeking expert help for those areas was actually the easy part. At home he was downright destructive. He poured out gallons of milk and a super-sized bottle of laundry detergent. If anything within his grasp was breakable, he broke it. Surviving meant childproofing our house and not letting Buddy out of our sight. There was always something to clean up, fix, or throw away. Following after him was like trying to clean up the aftermath of a tornado with a handheld vacuum. As someone who'd once taken pride in how I cared for my home and things, losing the ability to control both moved to the top of my grumbles list.

Buddy's five-year-old sister, Sissy, on the other hand, was bright and aware in so many ways, but her reactions to the trauma of her early years manifested in different problems. At least once a day, when Sissy faced an overwhelming emotion such as fear or anger, she would explode. Even though she was tiny in size, it took all my strength to contain her yelling, thrashing, kicking, and screaming—negative reactions she'd developed from her own fears and feelings of helplessness.

During her time in foster care, Sissy had been so difficult to handle she'd been moved numerous times within the system. To make things worse, right before we received Buddy and Sissy, both children had faced a failed adoption. They'd been told their "forever parents" had changed their minds about adopting them. No wonder they had backpacks full of bad habits and bad attitudes when they arrived. No wonder they had a hard time bonding with us. Even though it wasn't conscious, I'm sure their little minds and hearts were telling them, *Don't attach, because you're going to get moved anyway*. And I'm sure my own words confirmed that I wasn't going to keep them around—after all, my comments were mostly made up of grumblings about all they were doing wrong.

After a year of therapy—and a lot of work on John's and my part—these kids overcame much of that behavior. Amazingly, one of the tools we were taught to use was praise. It was my job, according to the therapist, to keep silent about all the things my kids were doing wrong and to loudly and excitedly praise even the small things they were doing right. Grumbling equals disconnection. And praise equals connection and bonding.

The tools our therapist gave us helped, and soon we started seeing positive changes. So much so that our lives found a new normal, and John and I decided to open our home again. This time we began the process of adopting four older sisters, also from foster care. I'd like to say that their issues were different from Sissy's and Buddy's. But they weren't. They were the same type of issues and responses, except bigger.

The destruction they exhibited and the huge reactions they had to the fear and anger they felt were familiar to us from our earlier experiences, but they came out in different ways. Pre-teens don't throw themselves on the floor and thrash; instead, they shoot their words at their targets like flaming arrows. They aren't drawn to spilling milk or laundry soap. Their destruction looks different, like twisting screens off windows and breaking picture frames and then spreading broken glass on the carpet.

You might be reading this section with wide eyes, and suddenly the grumbling that you've been struggling with doesn't seem too bad. The thing is, as our kids received the therapy they needed, they found healing, learned right responses, and discovered how to calm down, so smaller issues like grumbling became easy to ignore.

It would have been easy for John and me to look back at where we'd come from as a family and settle for "good enough." After all, good enough was great considering where we used to be. Yet for us, just surviving wasn't good enough, and settling wasn't good enough either. We wanted our kids to thrive. We wanted them to be loving, caring, giving, and thankful adults who didn't just grumble through life but instead became their best selves—who God uniquely created them to be—so they could impact the world for his glory.

John and I truly believe that God created each of our children with amazing gifts and talents that could be used to serve others and impact God's kingdom on earth. We'd overcome a lot of bad habits and trauma issues, and now it was time to focus on the smaller ones.

As our children grew in their relationships with God, it would be those little things that would hold them back—the things we often overlook. Yes, they could become missionaries, leaders, and diligent workers within our world, but these callings would be severely limited by discontented, unsatisfied hearts. Our job as parents was to help train and guide our children to overcome whatever was holding them back, which also meant overcoming whatever was holding us back.

It wasn't just the younger ones who were prone to grumble. John and (obviously) I battled with this, too, and so did our twenty-three-year-old son, Nathan, and my grandmother who lived in our home. My grandma was nearly ninety, but that didn't mean she'd figured it out. Often I'd overheard her mumbling under her breath, "Why did she get two cookies and I only got one?" No, grumbling doesn't stop just because you are older than Scotch tape, stop-action photography, and parking meters.

We'd committed as a family to this year of growth, and as I slowly moved past my own fear in order to pursue the discipleship I knew we all needed, it was time for the hard part of jumping in: launching out on the Grumble-Free Year.

John and I together came up with numerous ways to tackle this no-grumbling challenge, from creating a Gratitude Jar to memorizing Scripture to creating "Talk Chairs"—which was a place our children could invite us to if they needed to share something on their hearts. I had an idea that some of these things would work better than others, some might not work at all, or I might be surprised with what really stuck.

To make it through the year, it would take planning, coaching, leading, flexibility, and open hearts to each other and God. I'd never written a book like this before, one where I was not completely in control of what I would end up reporting within its pages. I had no idea what would come out of these kids' mouths! I had no idea what the year ahead would hold. Yet I trusted that if we were willing to take these first steps of preparing our hearts, God would show us the way.

Reflection Questions

1. In what ways do you struggle with grumbling?
2. In what ways does your grumbling spill over, impacting those around you in negative ways?
3. Why do you think it's easier just to survive every day rather than thrive?

4. How do you think your family members' small sins and struggles could impact their future work for God's kingdom?

5. What would it mean for each family member's future—including yours—if they overcame grumbling now?

Your Turn

Think back to a time when you let your grumbling thoughts turn into grumbling words. Do you often find yourself muttering between your teeth? I understand. Now think through how you could have handled that moment differently. Is there anything you could have done that would have brought peace, instead of conflict, to the situation?

Maybe like me, your grumbling somehow gives you a false sense of power when you truly feel powerless. When we grumble we often set ourselves up as a victim. Secretly we may hope that when others see us and hear us, they'll jump to our aid, but that never works. Consider what you can do instead of grumbling. I've often found that simply asking my family for help works better. It also teaches our kids how to act when they feel overwhelmed and need help too.

Finally, picture how you want your children to act as adults. How would you like their attitudes to be? How would you like to see them interacting with their own families? Make a pledge to yourself to model now the type of life you'd like to see them live as adults.

Part II

THE CHALLENGE BEGINS

Chapter 4

LET'S TALK ABOUT GRUMBLING

I decided that our very first day of homeschool would also be the first "real" day of our grumble-free year. For the last twenty-five years, I'd homeschooled my children. At the start of this school year, I was homeschooling seven of them. My youngest was almost seven and in first grade. My oldest daughter still at home was a senior. Yes, I was literally going to be teaching phonics and physics. Homeschooling can be overwhelming.

And that's the thing about homeschooling—or even parenting in general. There are so many big things that need to be taught that it's the real-life stuff that too often gets overlooked. When I'm focused on giving my kids the big overview of ancient history, I forget about teaching my kids about kindness. When we have a teen learning to drive (yes, we were doing that too), we're focused on finding an affordable car, making sure she understands road signs, and getting her used to all the huge semitrucks on the road.

And in the meantime I'm ignoring the signs that some of my kids are feeling unseen (which is a big problem in a big family). There is so much to teach the kids—and there always will be—that I was both terrified and excited to launch into this new teaching about grumbling (mainly how not to do it).

-¦-

Our first day of school had a few priorities. First, I focused on having a relaxing morning. I wanted to start the school year on a positive note. We took our time getting dressed and eating breakfast, then we launched into the most important thing: getting first-day-of-school pictures.

The mid-August sun shone brightly as my six kids lined up in front of the house. From the littlest one with light blond hair to the older girls with their dark brown hair to the light-haired little girls in the middle, everyone wore huge smiles. *Perfect.* What could be a better way to talk about grumbling than when everyone was in a good mood?

As we sat around the dining room table afterward, I told my kids that we were going to start our school day talking about the Grumble-Free Year.

"We're starting today?" Grace asked, indignant.

"Yeah, you should have warned us," Maddie protested.

"Are you taking notes?" Alexis looked to me, unsure.

I tapped the side of my head. "Right here. I'm recording everything right here."

Alexis wrinkled her nose. As the person she was counting on to make her famous, it didn't appear I was doing my job very well.

"And right here." I tapped the notebook beside me. "Don't worry. If you say anything brilliant, I'll write it down."

Alexis cocked an eyebrow. She was not convinced.

I smiled as I lifted up the white board where I'd written out Philippians 2:14: "Do everything without grumbling or arguing."

Nine-year-old Sissy's eyes grew wide. "Wait, we have to memorize that?"

I sighed. "Girl, I know your brain has been on a break with summer vacation, but this is only six words."

Laughter circled the table.

"I'll read it first, then you repeat after me."

I read it out loud, then the kids said it together a few times. Then each of them individually repeated it.

"Easy-peasy, right?" I scanned the table. "I give you all an A-plus."

"So are we all done?" I spotted seven-year-old Aly eyeing the new boxes of crayons, ready to christen our school supplies.

"Almost, but not quite. I'd like to talk about types of grumbling. Do you think grumbling is just the words we say?"

"Yeah, sort of." It was fourteen-year-old Grace again. She twirled a strand of dark brown hair around her finger. She was Maddie's twin and shorter by six inches. When we were in public she usually held back, so most people thought she was the quiet one of the two girls, but I knew that wasn't the case.

When I posed any questions in homeschool, Grace was usually the first to answer, whereas her older sister, seventeen-year-old Anna, rarely answered. Instead, Anna doodled on her notebook as we all talked. Even though it didn't appear like it, I knew she was listening. But I wanted to pay attention to her, to listen and encourage her too. Even though I was focusing this year on grumbling—and next year might be something different for the rest of these kids—Anna was going to college in the fall, and I really wanted her to get this.

"Anna, what do you think? Is grumbling only about our words?"

She glanced up at me. "Yeah, I think so. Maybe. Although sometimes it's more like mumbling, and you can't understand their words."

"That's a good point. But what about this?" I gave an exaggerated, unhappy sigh. "Do you know I'm not happy about something when I do that?"

"Yes!" the kids' voices cried in unison.

"So what are other ways of grumbling?" I paused and waited for their answers.

"Whining." Maddie shot a look at one of her younger sisters who was prone to that.

Her little sister crossed her arms and pouted, not happy about being called out.

"Yes, whining, but what about this?" I stood up and crossed my arms. "Whatever," I muttered. In my most dramatic fashion, I rolled my eyes.

"That's not grumbling!" Maddie proclaimed.

"Oh, yes, it is!" a few others chimed in.

And that's when I got an idea.

"Let's think about this another way. What are some things we're prone to do when we're unhappy?"

I wrote the words as they called them out: *whining, eye-rolling, mumbling, complaining.* And as I wrote each one on the board, we all came to the same realization: each of these ways of grumbling represented different members of our family.

I cleaned off my whiteboard, and we started a new list:

Complaining = Grace
Whining = Alexis
Muttering = Sissy
Criticizing = Anna

Moaning = all
Griping = Mom
Growling = Buddy
Protesting = Maddie
Fussing = Aly
Discontent = all

You would think that bringing up these faults would make everyone upset, but instead everyone became animated about their own manner of grumbling. A chorus of moans, groans, whines, and growls erupted. And as they "practiced," their faces filled with smiles.

It's as if they were truly seeing themselves and each other with new eyes. And all of us were realizing that we were doing a lot more grumbling than we first thought. It was just showing up in different ways.

As we talked, I knew we'd accomplished something significant. We were all more aware of ourselves, of our faults—which was new. Usually my kids focused on pointing out each other's faults over their own. I couldn't count the number of times a day my kids did that.

When they were doing their chores: "Look at the mess she made."

When they were trying to do homework: "Why is he being so loud?"

When anything was missing: "I didn't take it! She must have."

Everybody complained about each other. My kids were quick to judge, and yet they'd get upset when someone else pointed out their faults. This brought division between them nearly every day.

People don't want to be close to someone who is always pointing out their mistakes and not willing to own up to their own. Lately the fault-finding radar had gotten out of control, and that's why today was so surprising. Each person owned up to his or her own faults, and in doing that they actually started to understand themselves better.

This "owning up" was something I'd been trying to work on with my kids for years but to no avail. How many times had I pointed out when my kids did the very same thing they were complaining about? Too many to count.

But obviously that wasn't working. No one likes to be told they are wrong, and we all—my kids included—have a problem with admitting faults. The more I thought about it, the more I wasn't surprised. We're all insecure. None of us wants to be found out.

⁺

Deep down I knew why my kids were often afraid to admit their own faults. The main reason was insecurity, especially with our older girls. From the time they moved in they had been unsure of their place in our home, and it made sense. They had been moved around often in state care. And there had been many, many people who'd promised to give them a forever family before backing out on that promise.

In the first few days after they moved in, our older girls tried to do everything right. When they couldn't keep that up, everything flipped, and their behavior turned angry. They were so sure we were going to send them back. It was almost as if they were acting up so that we could send them back sooner, before they bonded with us. Every good day—a day when they felt a connection—was followed by three or four hard days. It took me a while to realize the pattern and to understand the root cause behind it. They'd draw close, feel insecure, then push away.

The weeks leading up to the finalization of our daughters' adoption were the hardest. Even on the day we were heading to the courthouse, one of our daughters mumbled all the way, "Something's going to happen. We're going to get in an accident or something." She was so sure that a forever family would fall through again, and when the judge finally declared, "You are now Goyers," the girls burst into tears.

I thought that insecurity would be a thing of the past once the adoption was finalized, but I hadn't realized how deeply rooted those feelings were.

Once, when I caught one of my daughters in a lie, I sat down with my preteen and said, "I know you did it. I don't want to argue any more about it. I still love you, and I always will. I just want to know why you felt you needed to lie."

The tightness of her jaw softened. Her eyes widened and rimmed with tears. And then the stories poured out of her about times in foster care and before. Every time she had done something wrong and been caught, she had felt unsure of what her consequences would be. Sometimes things would be shrugged off. Other times they'd be handled with extreme discipline. There'd been times when she'd been moved away from her sisters for her misdeeds. The more I listened to her stories, the more I understood why she wanted to hide—why she never wanted to admit her wrongs.

Which made today a breakthrough. My kids were able to look at themselves and admit their faults and know that they were fully accepted. What a great lesson for the first day of school.

⚡

Amazingly, all the kids were still in a good mood as I started the reading, writing, and arithmetic part of our homeschool day. More than once as we worked in our books and my kids started to complain, they'd catch themselves. And when my husband got off work, each of them wanted to share their grumbling styles with him. John was surprised, too, at how readily each of the kids accepted their own faults instead of simply pointing out each other's.

Over the coming week I was amazed how much they kept referring back to their grumbling styles. Not only did they tell their dad, they shared their styles with others too. And often when someone would start complaining, whining, or even growling, they'd catch themselves.

More than once a moody teenager gave me an eye roll and I pointed it out: "Oh, is that grumbling I see?" Many times—when I pointed to their go-to grumbling method—they'd relax and even joke along. Of course that didn't always happen. Too bad. It would have been great if the first week out we'd found the magic key that worked. But all the self-awareness and growth I did see on the front end gave me a good idea of how to help my kids next.

-¾-

In the early days of our adoption of Buddy and Sissy, I took both kids to therapy in hopes of helping their behavior improve. The truth was, they were getting a lot of attention for everything they did wrong. I followed them around from place to place, "No, don't do that. Stop!" I had no idea that my big responses were causing them to misbehave more because they thrived on attention—even negative attention.

The therapist urged me instead to stay mellow and provide

very little drama or energy when correcting my kids. And, in contrast, she wanted me to give over-the-board attention when they did something good. It makes sense. If someone praises me when I do something, it's a guarantee I'm going to do it again.

Now that I was aware of all of my kids' grumbling styles, this gave me a tool to use. Whenever I saw my kids starting to lean toward their grumbling style—and catching themselves—I started giving them high praise.

"Great job! I caught that almost eye roll."

"I noticed that you started to whine but then stopped. Good job."

Maybe you've learned this, too, but you've forgotten it in the daily grind of parenting. Praising someone for the good things they do does more to transform their behavior than pointing out what is wrong. This means pointing out even the smallest bit of good. It means noticing godly character even in our kids.

Sometimes we feel awkward praising our kids. We want kids to do what is right just because it's right and not because they are given a cheer and a handclap. Yet how are kids going to learn what is right if we don't make a big deal of it? Even Jesus affirmed others when they did things right.

One of my favorite stories is one that begins in Mark 14. While Jesus was reclining at a table in the home of Simon the Leper, a woman came with an alabaster jar of very expensive perfume, and she broke the jar and poured it over Jesus' head. While some of those who saw it were indignant that she would waste something so valuable, Jesus praised her. Mark 14:6–9 picks up the story:

"Leave her alone," said Jesus. "Why are you bothering her? She has done a beautiful thing to me. The poor you will always have with you, and you can help them any time you want. But you will not always have me. She did what she could. She poured perfume on my body beforehand to prepare for my burial. Truly I tell you, wherever the gospel is preached throughout the world, what she has done will also be told, in memory of her."

Jesus not only praised her, he also said that her deed would be repeated among others. And I've noticed that, while praising my kids means a lot to them, sharing the good things they've done with others—like their dad—means even more. When we see the character of God in our kids, we do need to take note of that.

Sam Crabtree, author of *Practicing Affirmation*, wrote:

> God-centered affirmations point toward the echoes, shadows, and reality of a righteousness not intrinsic to the person being affirmed. These qualities are gifts, coming from outside people and being worked in them. Even without yet being fully complete, these qualities are nevertheless commendable, and are to be seen and highlighted. We can truthfully say to an unregenerate four-year-old, "God is helping you become more . . ." and fill in the blank with qualities such as: careful with your things (as a steward), cheerful around the house as a singer, cautious around dangerous things like hot stoves, and so on. While the child's growth is commended, God is identified as the source.[1]

As the first few weeks of our grumble-free year passed, I worked to commend my kids for their self-control whenever they caught themselves grumbling and stopped. It became such a good opportunity to remind them that God can—and does—help them.

I didn't want to jinx myself by saying we were improving already, but I was so thankful we'd stumbled onto something that was showing results. It wasn't bad for the first few weeks. It was obvious my kids wanted to be understood. They wanted to be appreciated and praised, and they really wanted to do better. It was also a great lesson for me to learn.

Reflection Questions

1. What is your grumbling style? What are your kids' grumbling styles? Consider working together to find out.
2. Grumbling and blaming others often come from insecurities. In what ways have you seen this play out in your family?
3. What would happen if you focused on praising your children—even in the small things—instead of pointing out their faults?

Your Turn

Sit down with your family to figure out your grumbling styles. We found it to be a good experience. Because all of us were looking for our styles, no one person felt picked on. We all took note of our faults.

Are your grumbling styles whining, complaining out loud, or muttering under your breath? Remind your kids that God can help them not to grumble by giving them self-control.

Finally, be sure to praise your family members when they stop the grumbles. Praise their efforts and note when you see God providing self-control. Remind your children that they can turn to God often to help them more.

Chapter 5

LOOKING FOR
THE GOOD

One of my favorite things to do with my kids is reading aloud to them. Reading brings understanding of and empathy for people from all walks of life. It teaches my kids life lessons seen through a character's eyes. During our grumble-free challenge we started listening to the audiobook of *Pollyanna*. I'd never watched the movie or read the book before, but I was pleasantly surprised by how well it fit into our grumble-free year.

In the book Pollyanna is an eleven-year-old girl who is sent to live with a very negative, grumbly aunt named Miss Polly after the death of her father. Miss Polly is wealthy but bitter, and she sends Pollyanna to live in a small attic corner, away from the rest of the grand house. Pollyanna doesn't complain. In fact, concerning the room and everything else, Pollyanna looks for the good in things. Pollyanna plays what she calls the "Glad Game." No matter how difficult things are, she tries to find something to be glad about. My kids enjoyed the story, but when I asked if we should try the Glad Game in real life, they weren't as enthusiastic.

"You want us to do what?" Alexis asked, tossing her hair over her shoulder in a dramatic way. If there is one thing Alexis always is, it's dramatic.

The kids were again gathered around the kitchen table as we prepared for the school day.

"You know, play the Glad Game, like in *Pollyanna*. When we feel disappointed about something and want to grumble, we find something good about it instead."

I looked toward my youngest. Six-year-old Buddy looked back at me and raised his blond eyebrows.

"What?" I asked.

I looked toward my oldest. Seventeen-year-old Anna offered the same incredulous look. And all the kids in between seemed equally confused.

"What is it? The Glad Game is all about staying glad no matter what happens. It's something worth trying at least," I commented.

"What do you mean?" Aly wanted to know. Her round face peered up at me, and she wrinkled her nose, causing her scattering of freckles to bunch up.

"If it rains, for example, we can look on the bright side and say that we just have more time together inside."

"That sounds dumb." Sissy shook her head.

"No, it sounds optimistic."

"What does that word mean?" Grace asked.

"It means looking at things in a positive way."

The kids knew this was part of the Grumble-Free Year, and they liked Pollyanna, but they didn't think they could act the same way Pollyanna did.

"It's just a character from a book." Grace seemed unimpressed.

"But don't you think it's a good idea?" My smile brightened, and I clapped my hands together, trying to muster enthusiasm. "At least we can try."

"I guess so," Maddie commented. She tapped her pencil on the table as if asking, *Can we just move on to our real homeschool work now?*

"I guess we can do it if we have to," Grace added, showing her impatience. My guess is that both of them were only half listening. The twins' gazes met, and some type of secret conversation passed between them, one that didn't need words. Most of the time the twins had their own language that none of the rest of us seemed to understand, yet if they both were on board to play the Glad Game, then most likely the rest of the kids would follow.

"I'll do it because I'm amazing," Alexis said with a flourish. But the flourish didn't end up getting her very far. Though I reminded Alexis—and the others—throughout the day to try the Glad Game, we didn't do particularly well. Whenever someone complained about something and I reminded them to try to find one bit of good in the situation, I was mostly met by blank stares.

Maybe we were just trying too hard. Perhaps a fictional character wasn't enough inspiration. As I jotted down my notes, I was still trying to figure out what *would* be enough.

Even though we seemed to have hit a home run with figuring out our go-to methods of grumbling, things hadn't been going well since then. I was doing a lot of reminding about not grumbling, but there was less and less effort put in by my kids. One reason was simply us settling back into our old ways. I knew I needed to praise the good, but it was hard. My kids knew they needed to stop their grumbling, but that was even harder.

And while I knew this "grumble-free-ness" would be difficult, I never guessed how skilled my children would become at grumbling in creative ways simply in an effort to not put their grumbling into words. In addition to eye-rolling and heavy sighs, I saw stomping feet, squared shoulders, crossed arms, and slumping. A lot of slumping.

One day twelve-year-old Alexis was upset about having to stop her game-playing to do her chores. She put down her tablet, rose, and stomped across the room.

"You better calm down," my husband told her.

"I'm not saying anything." (Which, I admit, was impressive since this was the child prone to whining.)

"No, you're not saying anything," John replied, "but your actions are speaking loudly."

I made a note to myself: *We need to talk more about body language.* But I knew it also had to be more than that. Nothing was going to change if we only continued to teach about good and bad behavior. Instead, we needed to refocus on the heart—where all behavior stems from.

※

It had been an interesting start to the school year. In addition to spending many hours a day homeschooling, I also had a book launch, which sucked hours and hours of time from my afternoons for radio and podcast interviews. On top of that, five of my kids were still in occupational therapy, which amounted to three days a week of driving to therapy, which was about thirty minutes away. Thankfully I had some help. Our twenty-three-year-old son, Nathan, had taken some time off from college to write and publish his first novel, so he'd been helping me with the kids and with appointments. I'm not sure what I'd have done without him.

Even with help, though, it was a lot. I was still trying to figure out the balance of homeschooling so many kids and working from home—in a job with big deadlines that must be met. Since bringing home our four older girls, my office had moved to my bedroom, and I'd been cutting out more and more writing projects. I always liked to think I could do it all, but as balls dropped all around me it was clear I couldn't. Still, it was a hard lesson to learn.

Around that same time I was asked to write multiple books for a contract, and at first I excitedly said yes. Until I prayed about it. Then, deep down, I knew it wasn't something I needed to add to my life. As much as I loved writing, it was too easy to let it become my focus in an unhealthy way. When I wrote books, I could set goals and accomplish them. I could see the results of my work. Homeschooling and parenting didn't bring as much quick success, and I couldn't always see the rewards for my effort.

It was disappointing to say no to projects I wanted to do, and if I thought about it too much my heart could be filled with grumbles. Instead, I needed to trust that God could see what I couldn't. I was quite busy enough. And who knew what the future held?

So, even while I battled a bit of my own disappointment, it was time for us to return to the heart of grumbling. Working on this internally was the only thing that would help us externally. The Glad Game—forcing ourselves to try to be glad and find something good about every situation—wasn't working because it wasn't coming from deep in my kids' hearts.

The next day I sat down during our morning Bible time with a special story to share. I told the kids that the Bible referred to grumbling as "faithless complaining." Both the Old and New Testaments talked against grumbling, but there was one passage where God shared how truly serious it was to him:

> The LORD said to Moses and Aaron: "How long will this wicked community grumble against me? I have heard the complaints of these grumbling Israelites. So tell them, 'As surely as I live, declares the LORD, I will do to you the very thing I heard you say: In this wilderness your bodies will fall—every one of you twenty years old or more who was counted in the census and who has grumbled against me. Not one of you will enter the land I swore with uplifted hand to make your home, except Caleb son of Jephunneh and Joshua son of Nun.'" (Num. 14:26–30)

These were strong words. God called them a wicked community, and those who grumbled against him didn't enter the promised land—only those who believed did.

Both Caleb and Joshua believed that God would give them the promised land and that God would deliver their enemies into their hands. While the rest of the community saw the bad of the situation, namely the giants who lived in the land, Caleb and Joshua saw the good. They played the Glad Game, just like Pollyanna. And that's what faith is: trying to be glad and see the good because God is in control.

My kids listened intently, and I could see the wheels in their heads turning. *Surely my grumbling isn't that bad, is it? The Israelites had big things to grumble about; the things I grumble about are small.*

While my kids were still paying attention, I moved to the New Testament.

"God saw the grumbling as being against him. Jesus saw it that way too," I said. ""Stop grumbling among yourselves," Jesus answered.' That's in John 6:43. There are a few other verses I'd like to read too. Alexis, would you look up James 5:9?"

She opened her Bible, found the passage, and her eyes widened. "'Don't grumble against one another, brothers and sisters, or you will be judged,'" she read. "'The Judge is standing at the door!'" Then, with a dramatic gasp, she slammed the Bible shut.

"That's pretty serious, isn't it?"

The kids around the table nodded.

"Yeah, but they don't know my siblings," Maddie commented.

"Really? God doesn't know your siblings?" I chuckled. "I think he knows them better than you do, and the commandment still doesn't change."

I glanced at my paper and noted one more verse. "Anna, would you read 1 Peter 4:9?"

She found it and read, "'Offer hospitality to one another without grumbling.'"

"Does anyone know what *hospitality* means?" I asked.

"Having people over?" Grace responded.

"Yes, although it's sometimes easier being nice to people who come over for just a short time than to those we live with, isn't it?"

They all agreed it was.

I pushed my notes aside and noticed how fidgety everyone was getting. I also wondered if any of this was getting through. "Lately we've tried to do the Glad Game, like Pollyanna, but that really didn't work. After all, it's hard to act glad when we're still grumbling on the inside. And that's why I think our focus needs to be on something new. Every day we need to start praying for God to change us on the inside. We need to start praying for him to give us a thankful heart. True change will only come from the inside out."

We bowed our heads, and each of the kids prayed. Some took it more seriously than others, but every one of the kids prayed that God would help them be more thankful and not grumble all the time. It was a start.*

I prayed too. I prayed that God would help me change the most. "Lord, it's so easy to fall into bad habits. Help me do better so I can be an example. I know I can do it—we all can do it—with your help, Jesus."

Pollyanna may not be the best role model, but God could make the changes in our hearts. The thing was, we were going to have to turn to him more instead of depending on our own efforts. We were going to have to work on changing long term, for God's good, instead of focusing on what we wanted most in the moment. Would the kids be able to understand that?

In the desert God was asking his people, the Israelites, to give up the "security" of their barrenness to fight against an enemy in order to step into a land of abundance. The thing was, the barrenness was known, and the enemy was large and scary. And in an odd way, we'd become comfortable in our grumbling too. It was easier to act as we'd always acted (grumbling and all) than to put in an effort and join a fight against our own bad habits.

What was God asking us to give up? The right to ourselves. The right to say what we felt no matter how it sounded. No matter if it was mumbles and grumbles. No matter if our complaints actually highlighted not having everything we wanted and God not giving us everything we thought we needed. Ouch. Now I could see better how our grumbles impacted God, but I still struggled with how we could change.

We were real people with real heart struggles. As wonderful

as Pollyanna was, someone simply made her up in their mind, and real life has a tendency to be much more complicated than fiction.

Lord, what is it going to take to get through to our hearts?

Reflection Questions

1. What are your challenges when it comes to looking on the bright side of things? What are your family's challenges?
2. Do you ever try to make external changes without focusing on internal ones? Where does it get you? How does it make you feel?
3. It's easy to forget how seriously God takes grumbling. What stands out to you when you read God's message to the Israelites?
4. In the New Testament we are told that if we grumble, we will be judged. Why do you think grumbling matters so much to Jesus?

Your Turn

It's easy to see grumbling as a bad habit. It's harder to see that it is an actual offense against God. Even if we don't think so, it's saying, *God, you've failed me.* We may feel comfortable stuck in our grumbling, but God has so much more for us, just like he had for the Israelites. He had a promised land for them, but they only focused on the challenges and not on the good that awaited them. They refused to be glad that they were God's people—and that he had a wonderful plan for them—so they stayed stuck.

You can try playing the Glad Game. Maybe it'll work better for you than it did for me. And while that's worth the effort, I think more can be accomplished by reading these verses with your kids and discussing them:

- Numbers 14:26–30
- John 6:43
- James 5:9

After reading these verses, discuss with your family how grumbling is an offense to God. Together, pray and ask God to change your hearts. That truly is how all good changes must start.

Chapter 6

THE GRATITUDE JAR

I'm not a huge fan of Halloween. I don't like all the dark stuff, the scary stuff, the focus on evil. During the first twenty years of parenting, with our three oldest kids, I tried to ignore the day as much as possible. Instead, we made Halloween a family night. We had our own treats and watched a movie together.

But these younger kids—who'd spent time dressing up and trick-or-treating before they were adopted—weren't going to go for that. So we came up with a compromise. They could dress up in non-scary costumes, and as a family we'd go around the neighborhood and trick-or-treat with our neighbors. John and I considered it a time to get to know those who lived close to us better, and we had fun. But this year the days leading up to the big night seemed to bewitch all the kids. Maybe it was because their friends were already sharing candy with them. (Sugar overload!) Maybe it was because any big event tends to bring out anxiety in my kids.

In the past I'd talked to their therapist about the bad attitudes, disobedience, and mouthiness that happened before big events, and she said it was a form of sabotage. Because good things often didn't happen in their previous experiences, the kids had grown accustomed to being disappointed time and time again. So they often sabotaged a fun event because at least they were in control of it not happening.

That sort of made sense, but it also reminded me that, for our family, everyday life was hard enough. And taking on a grand goal, such as not grumbling, seemed almost impossible during weeks like this.

In addition to the stores being filled with Halloween items, Thanksgiving items were on display. Seeing all the "Give Thanks" plaques and decorations reminded me of something I'd wanted to do since I first thought of this book, and that was to create a Gratitude Jar.

Every school-day morning my kids and I still prayed that God would make us more thankful and less grumbly, and some days that worked better than others. John and I also made a list of the most common areas that resulted in grumbling—sibling conflict, not wanting to obey, chores, homework, screen time restrictions, and getting ready for bed—and we talked with our kids about these things, trying to help them understand how much easier it would be for everyone if they tried approaching them without grumbling. Again, some days it made more of a difference than others. Probably because, as parents, we weren't consistent in what we allowed or didn't allow, what we tried to correct, and what we let slide.

As I mentioned, our children grumbled in different ways, and, truth be told, some of the grumbles were more tolerable than others. For me, it boiled down to volume and attitude.

I wished this wasn't the case. But the truth was, it was easy for me to shrug off an under-the-breath grumble or complaint while the larger, more vocal displays caused the hair on the back of my neck to stand on end.

Seventeen-year-old Anna, for example, grumbled in a way I found more tolerable. She was one who kept her room fairly tidy and cleaned up after herself. Whenever she saw a spill she'd wipe it up, so when her younger siblings made messes, she complained a lot. That kind of grumbling didn't bother me so much. After all, I had the same complaints running through my head.

Anna especially had it hard because her room was a walk-through room that led to the very messy and out-of-control space where three of her sisters lived. This area used to be my office and library, and then it made sense to walk through one room to get to the other. But it didn't work so well for bedrooms, especially when three very messy teen girls regularly had to walk through the room of the neater one—and often left a trail of junk in their wake.

Anna had developed a habit of complaining about it daily. Either her sisters left their stuff behind or they messed with her things. Poor kid.

Yet it was still grumbling, right? And I did try to address it. "Why don't you just ask them to pick up the stuff they left in your room instead of grumbling about it?" I asked her.

"I do, Mom, but that doesn't make them stop. They don't listen and don't care. I'm tired of picking up their junk."

I talked to her three sisters again, and two of them promised to do better next time. Though, like Anna, I doubted this promise would last more than a few days.

But one of them, Alexis, simply found this to be a great time to argue about it. "I don't leave my stuff."

"You say that, but you have two pairs of shoes in your sister's room."

"Why are you only getting on me about it? Geez."

"I talked to your sisters, too, but you're the only one who is grumbling and arguing about it. Pick up your shoes, then head downstairs and write a note of thankfulness for the Gratitude Jar."

"What are you talking about?" She crossed her arms over her chest.

"Remember this morning when I showed you all that tall jar with a lid, and I told you that whenever someone grumbles, they need to write something they're thankful for and put it in?"

"Yeah, but other people grumble."

"Yes, and we'll deal with that when it happens. Right now I'm dealing with you."

She picked up her shoes and tossed them in her room and then just stood there, as if testing if I was really serious.

I pointed to the door leading downstairs. "Go ahead."

"I have to clean my room."

"Yes, I agree with that, but go write a gratitude first."

"This is stupid."

"That sounds like a grumble. Make that two gratitudes."

She stomped out of the room, calling back over her shoulder, "I'm not going to write anything for your dumb jar."

"That makes three gratitudes."

Her grumbling continued all the way down the stairs, and by the time we arrived in the kitchen she was up to nine.

I handed her nine slips of paper and a pencil. "Go ahead."

She stood there, silent, staring straight ahead. "I don't have anything I'm grateful for."

"Well, you either write them or you're going to bed now, with no dessert."

With a loud moan she took the pencil and began to write. She folded them up in small squares, not allowing me to see them, and dropped them in the jar. Then she stomped away.

I looked at the jar and those nine little pieces of paper and knew that hadn't worked like I'd wanted it to. It was a good idea, I supposed. But attempting to force someone to go from grumbling to grateful wasn't going to work. Sure, she complied, but only outwardly. There was no true gratitude deep in her heart.

I pushed the Gratitude Jar back on the counter and felt a sense of hopelessness. Was this just a big, dumb mistake? Was I going to put in all this time and effort and continue to fall short? Would there be any change by the end of the year? Would I look like a failure? I was a writer who gave parenting advice. I always liked to help and encourage other moms, but at this moment I needed a little help and encouragement myself.

As I looked at those wadded-up papers, part of me wanted to give up. Yet deep down I knew I needed to keep going. I was weary from the grumbles and complaints. I'd put so much into caring for these kids, and to hear them whine made me feel as if none of my efforts were worth it. I took their complaints personally.

I worried that maybe I wasn't giving and doing enough. I knew my kids were going to be adults someday. It was my job to train them. Grumbly kids and teens could turn into grumbly adults who were discontented and dissatisfied with life. I felt the weight of our current situation—and my kids' futures—on my shoulders, and it was a heavy burden.

How could I be a person who gave advice to other moms if I didn't have a grasp on this issue myself? There had to be something that would work.

We were in our third month of the challenge. We continued with Bible reading, focusing on scriptures that had to do with gratefulness and thankfulness, but my kids were rarely taking it to heart. I wished we'd made more progress by this point. While we all were better at understanding our grumble styles now, and I was giving lots of praise when my kids caught themselves grumbling and stopped, there was still plenty of grumbling to go around. And I wasn't sure what to do.

I wished I'd had some aha moment in which all the ideas I'd written down morphed into one doable plan, but the truth was, I felt half-hearted about our efforts myself. I'd gotten a Gratitude Jar because it had been on my list of things to do, but if this episode with Alexis was going to be typical of how things would go, I wondered if I really wanted to put the effort into making it work. At the moment, weary from the confrontation with my daughter, I didn't.

If only I could figure out the secret. I knew, during my quiet time the next morning, that I needed to start asking myself some serious questions. Maybe my heart—my motives—were the key to this whole thing. Maybe instead of trying to come up with good ideas that would help other moms, I needed to diligently start praying for my children, their attitudes, and all our interactions.

I also knew I needed to pay more attention to the "witching" hours, whether they were holidays or times of day. Attitudes tended to go south when kids were hungry or stressed, and I needed to be gentler when I was aware of this, helping my kids see some of the reasons behind their grumbles.

Cultivating a grateful attitude was not for the fainthearted. Lips that are quick to praise instead of grumble do not appear overnight.

It would have been foolish to believe I would be able to train my kids not to grumble and that they'd never be upset again. Being upset is a normal, natural emotion. And attempting to force positivity or gratitude would not get us very far. Instead, I had a feeling that the more I denied my children their upset emotions, the more these emotions would continue to build. And the more

I had unrealistic expectations, the more I'd be disappointed and frustrated.

As I was thinking of all these things, a scripture I'd memorized years ago came to mind. Psalm 19:14: "May these words of my mouth and this meditation of my heart be pleasing in your sight, LORD, my Rock and my Redeemer."

Maybe that's what had been missing. Maybe we'd been so focused on making the change for ourselves that we hadn't given as much attention as we should to God. The words we say either please God or they don't. The meditations or thoughts of our hearts also either please God or they don't. And even if all the kids did write notes for the Gratitude Jar, would they be doing it because I directed them to, or would they be doing it for God? I had a feeling it would be the former.

The question was, What could I do, as a mom, to encourage heart change rather than simply superficial change that we only thought was an indication of heart change? What could I do to guide my kids to desire to please God in all their actions and words? I was still trying to learn and grow in this myself. It was something to think about. It was something to pray about. Maybe, instead of looking around at more ideas for us to try, we needed to dig deeper and take a closer look at how our hearts were responding to God.

Reflection Questions

1. When are those "witching" seasons or hours with your kids? Do you know and understand times when they tend to grumble more? How can you prepare for these times?
2. Do you find it easier to handle some people's grumbles

more than others? What types of grumbles are most difficult for you to handle?

3. Has there been a time when you've tried to control another person, attempting to turn their grumbles into gratitude? What has been the result?

4. In what ways would your day be different if you directed your words, and the meditations of your heart, to be pleasing in God's sight?

Your Turn

I still think a Gratitude Jar is a good idea. I only wish I had handled it better. I was using the jar as a form of discipline: "If you grumble, you need to go write something you're grateful for instead." Yeah, that didn't work so well.

Henry Ward Beecher said, "Gratitude is the fairest bloom which springs from the soul." A seed of thankfulness must be planted before gratitude can grow, and no one is thankful when they're being disciplined, even if they know they're wrong.

Here's a better way to use a Gratitude Jar: encourage your kids to write notes of gratitude when they are already feeling grateful. Jot down your thankfulness on a piece of paper, then add it to the jar. The notes there will be true gratefulness, springing from the soul. And later you can all go back and read them, growing your grateful heart.

How can writing down gratitudes help? It is a physical way to celebrate a God-given emotion. Gratefulness is evidence of God working within our souls. Gratitude is an outpouring of what's inside, and taking note of our gratitude reminds our kids that when we are grateful there's someone we need to thank: God.

Chapter 7

WHEN LIFE GETS IN THE WAY OF OUR PLANS

It's humbling to realize the foolish way I believe I can get everything in order and organized today and then everything will magically stay the same way tomorrow. It's also humbling to see the way I apparently think I can figure out the order of my weeks and months and then just believe things will always work out as I'd planned, but it never does. Case in point: month four of our grumble-free year.

November started with plenty of unexpected surprises. Some good, some challenging.

A fun surprise was being asked to travel to Hollywood to be part of a media junket for the new animated Christmas movie *The Star*. As a blogger and podcaster, I traveled to Los Angeles, was put up in a swanky hotel, and interviewed the stars of the movie, including Patricia Heaton and Zachary Levi. Believe me, I had nothing to complain about.

But then I came home to some news. Now that Nathan had completed his goal of writing and publishing his first novel, he was moving into an apartment and getting a full-time job. This meant he wouldn't be working for me anymore, helping with the kids and driving them to their therapy appointments.

In the course of our family's adoption journey, Nathan had been the kid who'd had to adjust the most since he was the one still living at home. He became the dependable older brother the preteen and teen girls always wanted, and his bedroom soon became the hangout spot where they'd go to watch movies and eat snacks. He had an innate understanding of people. When I had been bent on getting our new kids on a chore schedule, Nathan had been the one who would sit and listen to the girls talk as they played video games together. He'd been such a gift. But now he was getting a new job, a new place.

As much as I was excited for him, I was sad to be losing my helper. I knew he'd still be somewhat available to the girls, but it wouldn't be the same. Also, I worried how I'd get my writing projects done once I lost those few hours of afternoon work time his presence had afforded me. Instead, I'd be driving my kids to their therapy appointments and managing the general chaos that comes with a large family.

Yet, as I considered the coming changes, my heart also flooded with thankfulness that I hadn't taken on those extra writing projects back in September. I was grateful I'd listened to God's still, small voice. I was thankful I'd said no. And now, in this new season, I looked toward Thanksgiving with a desire to truly be thankful, even if it meant this fall wasn't turning out like I'd hoped. God had other plans—I simply had to trust that.

—❅—

If there's ever a day to put grumbling aside, it's Thanksgiving Day. I'd done what I could to get the food ready to be cooked later that afternoon. This included peeling potatoes, prepping the turkey, and making desserts. I always try to do as much as I can the few days before Thanksgiving because we have a special tradition on Thanksgiving Day.

Since moving to Little Rock in 2010, we always spend the first half of Thanksgiving Day at our church, serving the community. We go to an inner-city church where a high number of people in the surrounding area live below the poverty line, so every year our church provides a community dinner and we feed over five hundred people. My husband, kids, and I always have the same job. We create a simple carnival with games, face painting, and treats for the kids. It's something we look forward to all year.

To make sure everything was in place in time, we had to be out the door early on Thanksgiving morning. This meant waking everyone up, getting them fed, and making sure everyone had shoes on. (More than once we've gotten someplace only to discover someone didn't have any shoes!) Yet when I got up that morning, I quickly realized something was wrong. My body ached and I felt horrible. I had a fever, and all I wanted to do was climb back into bed. I attempted to get up, but my legs were shaking. Worries filled my mind. There would be no way I was going to church to serve others, let alone finish cooking all the food for Thanksgiving.

I managed to get up to tell the kids to get dressed, and when I got back to the bedroom John could tell things weren't good.

"I'm not going to be able to go . . . I feel awful," I said as I climbed back into bed.

"Then we'll have to cancel the carnival." Panic filled my husband's face. "There's no way I can manage watching all our kids and running all the games."

"Don't worry. I'll text Pastor Harry and ask if we can get more help—"

I hadn't finished my sentence when a loud crash sounded from the other room. John and I looked at each other.

I gasped. "What was that?"

John jumped to his feet. "It sounds like a bookshelf got knocked over . . . or something else big." We rushed to my grandma's bedroom and opened the door. Grandma lay on the floor. Fear gripped me, and I rushed to her.

"Grandma, what happened?"

She looked at me, bewildered. "I don't know . . ."

She was half-dressed and looked dazed. "What am I doing down here?" She reached for her head. When she pulled her hand away, I noticed there was blood. I grabbed a blanket and covered up her bare legs.

Hearing the commotion, the kids came running from all over, peering in the door of her bedroom.

"Grandma, what's wrong?"

"Is she okay?"

"What happened?"

I rushed to the bathroom and grabbed a towel, placing it on her head. She still couldn't tell us what had happened or why she was on the floor. She was talking, but she didn't make sense. This didn't look good.

My grandma moaned, and I turned to John. "We need to call 911. She might need to be taken to the hospital. This could be serious."

The community event at our church, Thanksgiving dinner—neither of those seemed important now. My fever and aching body didn't either. I simply needed to make sure my grandmother was okay.

The firemen and EMTs arrived within ten minutes. They checked Grandma over, took her vitals, and helped her to her feet. She was a little wobbly, but she was able to walk back to her bed with help. The wound to her head was small, but it had bled a lot. The EMTs cleaned the area and bandaged it up.

"I think she's all right, ma'am. Her vitals look good. Probably just tripped on something and went down. I think she'll be okay today, but you probably want to make an appointment with her doctor within a few days to get her checked out."

"Yes, I will. Thank you."

I helped Grandma get cleaned up and settled into bed. She was talking much more clearly now. She even asked for a Popsicle. I took this as a good sign. As she settled in, the aches from my fever came upon me again. With all the strength I had left, I got a Popsicle for my grandma and then staggered back to bed.

John got ahold of our pastor, and Pastor Harry promised helpers for the carnival and to help watch over all our kids. For the next three hours, while John and our kids were serving at church, I went back and forth between checking on my grandma and attempting to keep my fever down.

Around the same time my family arrived home from church, Kayleigh showed up with her kids. Kayleigh is our unofficial daughter. She is one of the teen moms I'd started mentoring in 2002, and she had started spending more and more time with our family outside of the teen mom support meetings. When our family moved from Montana to Arkansas in 2010, Kayleigh and her three kids did too. She's our daughter in every sense except for taking our name.

With me still in bed, Kayleigh took over directing the preparation of Thanksgiving dinner while the kids took turns watching Grandma and helping her. Grandma seemed to be doing all right except for still being unsteady on her feet. John got out her walker and insisted that she use it. She'd had the walker for years but had been too independent to use it. Now it seemed she had no choice.

This wasn't the Thanksgiving I had planned, but as I heard my family gathering around the dining room table, thankfulness filled my heart. My grandma wasn't hurt seriously. Kayleigh had stepped in to cook Thanksgiving dinner. This day wasn't anything like I'd planned, but it could have been worse. Truly there was nothing to grumble about.

⸳⸰⸳

The mantra that filled my mind on Thanksgiving Day continued to replay in my thoughts for the weeks to come.

The house is a horrible mess . . . but I have nothing to grumble about. We have a home.

Homeschooling was hard today . . . but I have nothing to grumble about. I'm thankful we have the opportunity to teach our children at home. I'm thankful they are growing and learning.

Grandma is slowing down . . . but at least the doctor says he doesn't think there was any serious damage done.

Day by day, the more I told myself, *I have nothing to grumble about,* things began to change. Life didn't get easier, but my heart began to soften. Things that used to bother me didn't bother me as much. I'm not sure if the kids noticed, but I did. *Thank you, Lord.*

Looking back, this was God's grace to me because, added on

to everything else, a truly hard season of caring for Grandma was right around the corner.

The first time I took Grandma to the doctor, he said he didn't have the right equipment to examine her, so he sent us to the emergency room for them to take a closer look at her back. She'd been complaining about her tailbone hurting since the fall, and I did my best to keep her comfortable. But it bothered me that she hardly wanted to get out of bed.

At the ER, they found she had a urinary tract infection, which can cause pain, but they said they couldn't see anything wrong in her back except that she'd had an old injury. I took her home again, but as time passed and she continued to slow down, my worries grew. I did everything I could to try to keep her comfortable. I alternated both heat and cold on her back. I massaged it with an electric massager and gave her over-the-counter pain meds, but nothing seemed to help.

A few weeks later we went back to the doctor and then back to the emergency room. This time the MRI uncovered something the X-ray had missed. Grandma did have a fracture from her fall, and they wanted her admitted to the hospital immediately. My heart ached. My poor grandma, eighty-eight years old, and she had been walking around with a broken back!

This time of year was always busy enough, especially with the decorating, shopping, cleaning, and cooking for our big family. But I was spending large parts of my day at the hospital. Thankfully my kids were on break, and I didn't have to worry about homeschooling.

See, I have nothing to complain about, I'd tell myself as my kids poured themselves more cereal for breakfast and I rushed to the hospital to be with Grandma. Friends took turns checking in on my kids when they could, and John worked from home, so he was around to help too.

I'd sing praise songs on the way to the hospital, but when I got there, worries soon replaced my thankful attitude. My grandma had dementia but did well at home with her familiar surroundings. Unfortunately, in the hospital she became disoriented and confused.

The care staff at the hospital talked about putting Grandma in a rehabilitation center for at least a few weeks while she got stronger, but warning signals went off in my head. She was so disoriented now that there were times she didn't recognize me and she didn't know who I was talking about when I mentioned her daughter or other family members. The only thing that perked Grandma up was a visit from my little kids. So deep down I knew the best thing for her was to bring her home, no matter how much work it would mean for me.

And it was a lot of work. After a week in the hospital, my grandma was so weak she couldn't get out of bed on her own. But since she had dementia, she didn't remember that she couldn't get up, so she'd try, straining her back, which was doing more harm than good.

The solution was to put up a motion sensor attached to the wall next to her bed. Every time one of her arms or legs would stretch beyond the bed, an alarm would beep, alerting me. Then I'd go in there and help her, reminding her that she couldn't get up. This happened up to five times a night and all through the day. I was exhausted, but my heart was at peace.

I had nothing to grumble about. My grandma was still with me, and we were all going to be together for Christmas.

And as for the Grumble-Free Year, I told myself we'd get back to that after the New Year. This wasn't the holiday season we had planned, but my kids understood. In fact, was it just my imagination, or were my kids grumbling less?

-☀-

Maybe, like me, you're facing a hard season. They come unexpectedly, and the challenges pile up in our already busy lives. The thing about hard seasons is that we never know when they're going to end. Challenges build upon each other, and often these challenges aren't things we can fix. We can't fix broken backs. We also can't fix lost jobs or bring instant healing to broken relationships. And we can't always discover the right answers. Yet there is one thing we can seek, and that is wisdom.

James 1:5 says, "If any of you lacks wisdom, you should ask God, who gives generously to all without finding fault, and it will be given to you." Caring for an injured eighty-eight-year-old was hard and full of questions. How could I give my grandma my best and do what was best for my family too?

Yet, as I prayed about it, I had a profound sense that caring for my grandma well was the best thing for my family. Not every child has a great-grandmother living in their home. Deep down I knew my kids would learn how to love and care for others by seeing me love and care for Grandma.

And it was no coincidence that the message God had planted in my heart, even before Grandma's accident, was "nothing to grumble about." It was something God was working within my heart. He wanted me to focus on the good things, no matter how small. In a season when I didn't have a lot of answers, God gave me wisdom.

Reflection Questions

1. When was a time you made plans and then life got in the way, changing everything?
2. Has there been a hard time in your life when you decided to approach it with thankfulness? How did things change when you looked at the experience through grateful eyes?
3. When was a time the pain or challenges of others caused you to be thankful for your own circumstances?
4. Can you think of a season when God was with you as you helped another person through a challenging time?

Your Turn

Consider jotting down this phrase on a sticky note and posting it around the house: "Nothing to grumble about." It's a reminder that no matter how many challenges there are, we can always find something to be thankful about. And through life's challenges we're often taken back to what really matters.

As pastor Rick Warren says, "The Bible is very clear that God put you here on Earth to do two things: to learn to love God and to learn to love other people. Life is not about acquisition, accomplishment, or achievement."[1] This quote makes sense, but it's hard to do unless you get to the point when it's the only thing that can be done. When you can't acquire, accomplish, or achieve, then it becomes easier to love God and love others. And sometimes that's what our kids need from us most—to simply show them how to be thankful when life is hard and how to love when we're overwhelmed, tired, and it's not easy to do.

Chapter 8

WHAT REALLY MATTERS

There aren't many fun things about being in foster care, but if my kids could pick one "best" thing, Christmas would be it. During the Christmas season, people usually think more about others, and often they think about foster kids who aren't with their biological families or their forever families. Generous people are often happy to purchase gifts for foster kids when they are out shopping. This meant that when my kids were in the foster system, they could make a list of things they wanted, and they were guaranteed they would get the items on their lists. Telescopes, microscopes, sleeping bags, iPods, Kindles . . . their lists were long, and they received everything they asked for and more. Christmas was celebrated multiple times at the children's home where they lived and at churches and through other organizations as well.

When John and I brought our kids home, we were thankful people had loved our kids so well. A problem arose, however, when their first Christmas with us neared.

"Mom, I want a leather jacket and boots," Grace told John and me.

"Oh, I want that too," Maddie chimed in. "And makeup. Nail polish too." And the list went on and on.

"We'll see," I told them. I was making a note of some of the things they wanted, of course, but I also knew John and I had a limited budget. With ten kids, grandkids, and extended family, we'd have to choose well.

In the month before Christmas, each of the older girls brought me a list.

"We'll see what's possible," I told them each time.

But as Christmas neared, I noticed they paid extra attention to the boxes under the tree.

"Mom, do you have more gifts in your room?" Alexis asked one day.

"No, I've put them all out."

"Does Dad have stuff that he's hiding?"

"No." I shook my head. "Dad and I buy things together."

"But that can't be all of the stuff on our lists," she told me.

"Well, it's not. Dad and I don't have enough money to buy everything on your list."

Panic filled her face. "Well, can you call our social worker and see if we're getting gifts from them too?"

"Honey, even though the adoption isn't final yet, I don't think anyone else will be buying you presents. You're with us now."

Word got out among the sisters, and they all came to me with equal concern.

"We're not getting everything on our list?" Grace asked.

"No, honey. We have a lot of kids. We can't afford that."

"Are we getting gifts from DHS?"

"No, I don't think so."

"Can you ask?" she pleaded.

I called the social worker that day, and she confirmed what I thought. "No, they're with their forever family now. They won't be getting gifts from us."

I told the girls what their social worker had said, and I noted a hint of disappointment on their faces. Yet I still had high hopes that the family gathering Christmas morning would mean more than the things they received or didn't receive.

Even with items piled halfway up around the tree, the presents didn't go as far as you'd think when spread out among twenty people. The girls tried to be happy, but I didn't miss the disappointment on their faces.

"Is that all?" I heard one sister comment to the other after we were finished opening gifts. Part of it broke my heart, but I also wished my children could be more thankful—and not grumble. After all, we were doing our best.

Even though two years had passed since that time, Christmas gift shopping still brought me anxiety. I always tried to balance purchasing things I knew my kids would love with what we could afford. But this Christmas was even more difficult. I hadn't shopped as much as I'd wanted to. I hadn't baked at all. Yet, amazingly, the thing everyone was excited about was having Grandma with us. She'd been released from the hospital just days before Christmas, and even though she was still weak, her smile was bright. She sat in her back brace on a rolling office chair while we read the Christmas story, and she was able to watch the kids open a few gifts before having to go rest in her room.

The kids received less than previous years, and far less than they had in foster care, but I saw more gratitude this year than I'd seen before. We were supposed to be working on the Grumble-Free Year, but because of Grandma's health challenges, working on this project had been put on the back burner. But watching someone we loved go through so much made us all look at things differently. The items mattered less this year. The people mattered more. We'd found a bit more thankfulness, just in a way we didn't expect.

What a sweet gift, I whispered to God. *Thank you.*

⛭

My grandma's broken back wasn't anything we'd expected. Before her fall, we had a very busy life. John worked full-time from home and was a children's leader at church. He often had to travel for work too. I had books to write and kids to homeschool. My children had therapy appointments, and we all had church responsibilities. And then the holidays always added extra work, extra events.

Yet crisis doesn't call ahead to see if you have time for it. Disaster doesn't do rain checks if it's not a good time. My grandma's brokenness reminded us of what really mattered. It caused us to pause and recall that the whole reason for God coming to earth was man's brokenness, in body, soul, and spirit.

If this world had its act together, there would be no need for Christ. And because things had been broken in our home—our routines and normalcy—we all had to pause from considering ourselves and think more of others.

Grandma received extra care, of course, but I was touched to see my kids extend the same tenderness and thoughtfulness to each other. Kids pitched in to help me more, and there was far less striving in search of the perfect Christmas.

A synonym for *crisis* is *turning point*, but sometimes we forget that. For us the turning point was when we came face-to-face with the fact that life is fragile. Even though my grandma was in her late eighties, we'd taken her for granted. She'd always been around, and, for the most part, she'd always been healthy. She'd been slowing down physically, and dementia had robbed her of her short-term memory, but she'd been just as sassy as ever. Then one fall one busy morning changed everything. Just like everything changed the day Jesus was born. There were lots of interruptions on the first Christmas. As Max Lucado wrote:

> Off to one side sits a group of shepherds. They sit silently on the floor, perhaps perplexed, perhaps in awe, no doubt in amazement. Their night watch had been interrupted by an explosion of light from heaven and a symphony of angels. God goes to those who have time to hear him—and so on this cloudless night he went to simple shepherds.[1]

For the shepherds, their night watch had been interrupted. For us, our busy, self-focused lives had also been shaken up. Caring for a bedridden grandma was too much to add to a busy home. Or was it? The glitz and the glam of a Hallmark holiday paled in comparison to a weak but happy smile of a sweet grandma. The kids received gifts and enjoyed them, and even though they didn't get most items on their lists, that no longer mattered. Or at least, if they did grumble about it, it wasn't in my earshot.

If we had to schedule turning points, we never would—who wants to schedule a crisis? Yet maybe they're what we need once in a while, just to get everyone focused on what really matters.

Reflection Questions

1. How have unrealistic expectations put a damper on your past holidays?
2. Once we go through hard stuff, we often learn to appreciate the simple things in life more. When has this been true in your life?
3. In what ways has your family found gratitude and thankfulness during times they didn't expect?

Your Turn

Write down a list of things you've discovered really matter in this life. Your list may include things like family, friends, having meaningful work, and health. Then write down times when you learned these lessons. Most of the time these teaching moments happened in the course of life.

Next, share about these challenging times with your kids. Then ask them to share times when they also learned important lessons. Sharing stories highlights what truly matters instead of what we feel we're still lacking.

Chapter 9

PRAISE HARDWIRED

Weeks passed before I remembered that I was supposed to be guiding my children through a grumble-free year. Our lives had been singularly focused on one thing: taking care of Grandma. In the three weeks since Grandma had been home, I'd become consumed with visits from therapists, caring for her needs day and night, and filling out paperwork to receive home health care.

"Therapy's here!" Sissy called from the dining room table as the occupational therapist arrived, right on schedule.

I handed our read-aloud book to Anna. "Can you finish reading this chapter for me?" It was her senior year, and this wasn't how things were supposed to look. I'd planned on lots of coffee dates to talk to my beautiful daughter, imparting truth and wisdom while I had the chance. Yet since I was waking up five times a night (jumping up whenever Grandma's alarm went off), I could barely keep my eyes open throughout the day, let alone attempt to be wise. And instead of planning parties with her fellow homeschooled classmates, after completing her own work, Anna was quick to help me with the other kids and their homeschooling work.

As I hurried to the front door, a voice echoed from behind me. "Grandma, you can't get up. Sit down right now." Maddie's voice was kind but firm. "Mom! Grandma's not listening to me."

"I'll be right there . . ." I answered the door. With a smile I welcomed the therapist in. "I think she's trying to get up. She has no idea she's not stable enough for that yet—or the strain she's putting on her back. She just doesn't remember."

"Yes, that's the problem." He sighed. "As we help her get stronger, it'll be harder to keep her from hurting herself, especially since she doesn't remember she's injured in the first place."

I hurried into my grandmother's bedroom, which was near the front door, and rushed to Maddie's side. My fifteen-year-old was still trying to get Grandma to sit back down on her bed, to no avail.

"Grandma, you have to sit down," Maddie repeated, clearly frustrated, fists pressed into her hips.

"But I have to go potty!" Grandma's voice rose. "I've got to go."

"It's okay, Maddie. I got this," I told her. "Go back and listen to the story."

"Grandma." I placed a soft hand on her arm as I heard the footsteps of the therapist behind me. "You need to sit down so we can get your back brace on. You have to put it on before you get up, remember?"

Even though Grandma had been wearing a back brace for a month, she'd forget about it every time. Every day was like the movie *Groundhog Day*, a repeat of the day before. Sometimes I'd be so exhausted that I'd sleep through the alarm that alerted me to Grandma trying to get up, and John would have to shake me to wake me up.

"Trish, Grandma needs you," he'd tell me.

"Okay," I'd moan as I stumbled out of bed.

It was the alarm that had alerted Maddie to Grandma's movement. With all the kids in the house, someone was always there to remind Grandma to sit until I could help her.

I picked up the back brace. "Here, put your arms up."

"I don't want to put that on. I have to go to the bathroom."

I felt the therapist's hand on my shoulder.

"Here, let me do that." He smiled. "Ms. Coulter, I'll help you get that on. Then let's see how well you can walk to the bathroom today."

I took a step back, thankful that this time I had help—at least with getting the brace on and helping her walk. Most days I was doing it myself, and it was hard not to grumble, at least on the inside, especially in the middle of the night.

Last month I had been thankful that I was able to bring Grandma home from the hospital. This month I was still thankful for that, but I was getting weary.

Oh, Lord, I prayed often, day and night. *I don't feel as if I have anything left in me. How am I going to teach the kids about not grumbling when I'm exhausted from daily life?*

I wish I would have received a clear answer. Wouldn't it be nice if a No Grumbling curriculum showed up on my bookshelf next to all the rest of the homeschooling curriculum? It didn't, of course. This was a journey I was on with God, attempting to seek his face as I tried to guide my kids. The thing was, it took me a while to realize that he was actually sending clear lessons in the midst of our circumstances.

After the therapist left and Grandma was again settled down in her bed, propped up with pillows and her back brace off, something else interrupted our homeschooling lesson time. This time it wasn't a visit from a therapist. Instead, it was singing.

"What is that?" Grace asked, turning her head toward Grandma's bedroom. "Is she playing music?"

"Actually, it's her. Grandma's praising Jesus."

I immediately recognized the sweet soprano voice I remembered from my childhood. I always liked to sit next to my grandma in church growing up, mostly because I loved to hear her sing. She didn't have the prettiest voice in church. No one ever asked her to sing a solo or join the choir, but it was beautiful to me. She'd lift one hand as she lifted her voice. Her eyes would be closed too. Many times she wasn't reading the projected words on the wall but instead was mixing in her own praises, singing to Jesus from deep in her heart.

And that's what she was doing this day too. Grandma sang with a mix of lines from her favorite hymns and her own praises and thanksgivings to God. Yes, thanksgiving. Even as she lay propped in bed with an aching back and limited mobility, she thanked God. She thanked him for life. She praised him for his goodness. Her praises didn't erupt because of all the wonderful things happening in her life in that moment. Instead, they sprouted from a heart that understood God was worthy to be praised, no matter what. Grandma knew her praises were about him and not her situation. She sang because she was thankful for life, no matter how frail her body was. More than that, she was thankful for the eternity to come: an eternity without an aging body, pain, or confusion. She sang about that too.

As I listened I realized all the kids were listening too. I could tell from their furrowed brows that they were trying to make out her words.

"She's thanking God. Singing to him." Maddie smiled.

"Sometimes, in the middle of the night, I wake up to hear her praying aloud, thanking God for all he's done for her," I told them. "She also prays when she is hurting and her body doesn't move the way that she wants it to. In fact, when she's really hurting, she prays in Spanish."

"Spanish!" Buddy shouted the word as if it were the most amazing thing he'd ever heard.

"Why Spanish?" Aly asked.

"Well, that's what she learned to speak first." I paused, realizing how little I'd told the younger kids about Grandma's life. "Her parents were immigrants from Mexico, and they spoke Spanish. Her mother never really did learn English her whole life."

"Tell them about the boxcar, Mom." Grace's head bobbed. More than any of the other kids, Grace often liked to spend time in Grandma's room, watching movies with her and asking her stories about her life.

"What boxcar?" Buddy again exclaimed.

I settled into my chair. "Grandma was born during a time called the Great Depression. Her family actually turned a small boxcar into a house, and they lived in that for all her growing-up years. Grandma, her two brothers, and her parents in that little space. Well, until her father died when she was just eight years old. Things got even harder after that." I stopped there.

I could see this was difficult for the younger kids to take in. They were used to their great-grandma sneaking cookies and telling them to stop running in the house. Yet she'd been a little girl who faced challenges just like they had. And as an adult, things hadn't gotten easier. As a young mother of three children she'd once become so ill her family was told she wouldn't make it through the night, and yet here she was. Had all those years of hardship changed her heart? Had she learned to praise instead of grumble as the chapters of her life filled with both joy and hardship? Was this my lesson now?

"Yeah, we have nothing to complain about," Grace mumbled. Then she turned her attention back to the homework in front of her.

"You know, I was thinking the same," I responded.

"Can Sissy and I watch a movie with Grandma when we're done with our homework?" seven-year-old Aly asked, brown eyes large and round as she looked up at me. Aly could be just as loud as the other kids, but she could also be quiet and sweet. Her love language was quality time. I knew this gesture was a way to connect with her great-grandma and to show her love.

"Yeah! *The King and I*," Sissy piped up. "Or maybe *The Unsinkable Molly Brown*. That's her favorite."

"Of course you can. Let's hurry and finish this." I smiled. And as I returned to the lesson, I realized that, although I'd fallen short at trying to work on this grumble-free thing, God had been working on it all along.

What other kids had such an example of a great-grandmother's faith shining strong, even in the midst of hardship? Yes, Grandma grumbled at times, especially when her television wasn't loud enough or when the therapist wanted her to do five more arm lifts than she wanted to do, but, as everyone saw, the core of her heart was one of thanksgiving. She'd walked enough steps on this earth to become familiar with drawing close to God and leaning on him. When she couldn't remember much of anything else, she remembered this.

⫶⚬⫶

I wish I could say my grandmother's faith buoyed my own 100 percent of the time, but these were some of the hardest days I'd ever faced. When we first brought her home, I'd had to change her diapers, and when she got a little stronger, I had to put on her back brace and lift her, helping her to the potty beside her bed. It was like having a 150-pound newborn who needed constant attention.

To help with that, I found two programs that would assist us with my grandmother's needs. One of them would offer us supplies and help with at-home care, and a second would provide extra at-home care hours. The only problem was, the second program needed to be paid up front and we'd be reimbursed later. To get help for those extra hours, we needed $3,000 right away.

John and I tried to keep a small savings, but unexpected challenges, like losing our microwave, dishwasher, washing machine, and dryer in a few months' time, had put a large hole in our funds—not to mention Christmas and the daily care of eleven people in our home. To put it simply, the money just wasn't there.

Needing these services, yet not having anywhere to turn, I sought prayer from a group of writer friends I met with every year. We'd prayed each other through much over the years, including the death of parents and the death of a spouse, and now it was my turn to ask them to pray.

One of my prayer sisters did more than just agree to pray. She started a GoFundMe page, seeking money for our need. I was overwhelmed with gratitude!

Within a week, the GoFundMe page was shared 438 times, and sixty-two people donated. My heart swelled with thankfulness, and when the bill came, the money was there. As someone who'd always taken joy in helping and providing for others, God showed me that sometimes he could best meet my needs through the love and care of others.

※

December had come in as a perfect storm: Nathan quitting his job as a "manny" and moving out. Having no babysitter, which meant no time to work. Grandma falling, hurting herself, and needing constant care. It had also been a hard few months for our family's health. One person after another got sick. One thing followed by another.

Then there was the book about angry kids that I was editing (*rewriting* would be a more accurate term). There were marriage problems with close family members that broke my heart and kept me up at night in prayer. (Who am I kidding? I prayed for this family as I woke up numerous times every night with my grandmother.)

Yet, even in the midst of this, thankfulness filled my heart. It was hard to grumble when my grandmother rejoiced. She was a vivid reminder that praise comes out of a thankful heart, not our circumstances. And when we have people to love and care for us, we have everything.

How amazing that my grandmother forgot her major injury day after day, yet there wasn't one day when she forgot how to praise. Daily, no matter her pain, no matter her frustration over her loss of mobility, she'd lift her voice and lift her hands. But the praise didn't start with this storm. Grandma's praise had been lifted up through every peak and valley she'd journeyed through in the last forty years since she became a Christian, and through this daily habit of gratefulness—instead of grumbling—praise had been hardwired in.

In addition to the prayers and financial gifts of friends, so many of our other needs were met too. My kids' therapists came to our home for their sessions since I couldn't leave. Friends from church brought dinner a few times. Other friends gave the kids rides to their youth group and American Heritage Girl meetings. I even had a friend who babysat Grandma twice in one week so I could go out with the whole family when my daughter Leslie and her husband, Honza, were visiting from the Czech Republic.

During this time I also thought about what I had learned from my life coach: to focus on the good. To repeat thankfulness instead of grumbling. It made even more sense now. It's what Grandma had done. And it was now what kept her strong. And so I practiced.

God was taking care of us.

I had enough time to do all God had called me to do.

I couldn't grumble . . . I had nothing to grumble about.

Thank you, Lord, for loving me in the moment just as I am.

As I witnessed my grandmother's faith, John 15:16 came to mind: "You did not choose me, but I chose you and appointed you so that you might go and bear fruit—fruit that will last—and so that whatever you ask in my name the Father will give you." My grandmother didn't live an adventurous or extravagant life, but she loved God and loved others well. She had borne fruit, fruit that had lasted far into her old age.

As I pondered this during my morning quiet time, I also came across this quote: "God can do nothing for the man with a shut hand and a shut life. There must be an open hand and heart and life through which God can give what He longs to give."[1]

Grandma had cared for me when I was young. She had opened

her hands, opened her life. And now I was happy to do the same. And through giving I was receiving—and my children were receiving—what God longed to give: grateful, thankful hearts.

Even though the days proved to be difficult, my kids were spending more time with Grandma than they ever had. And as they sat there and watched movies with her, I knew they were making memories. These were times they'd never forget. And hopefully lessons they'd never forget too.

Maybe we'd all do well to remember that it's the hard seasons that teach the greatest lessons, especially when we walk through those seasons with someone who knows how to turn to God for strength.

Reflection Questions

1. When is a time God provided unexpectedly? How does thinking of that make you thankful now?
2. In what ways can you hardwire praise, instead of grumbling, into your life?
3. Who in your life is (or can be) an example of faith, even during hard circumstances, to you and your children?
4. How will having an open hand and open life allow God to give what he loves to give?

Your Turn

Sometimes we don't like to share our struggles with our kids. We want them to believe we have our act together. First, because we don't want our kids to worry. Second, because we want to feel as if we are the ones our kids can depend on. But is dependence on us really the most important thing?

I felt weak telling my kids that we didn't have enough money to cover Grandma's caregiving expenses. I felt feeble fumbling through daily life with the newly added responsibilities—and I couldn't hide it from my kids. They saw the bags under my eyes and the constant yawns.

Yet my kids also saw how others stepped forward to help, and I let them know how time and time again God provided. Instead of wondering why this had to happen, I found small ways to be grateful, just as Grandma was showing me.

Take some time today to be honest with your kids about your struggles. Then share all the ways you've turned to others and to God for help. Finally, share the unexpected blessings you've found along the way. And as you do this, your kids will also learn that it's okay to turn to others and to God for help.

Chapter 10

MINDFUL DECISIONS

Things couldn't have worked out more perfectly as spring approached. We received the assistance we needed when we hired Kayleigh to be Grandma's caregiver in our home. Kayleigh, who as I already said was like a daughter to me. Kayleigh, whom Grandma was used to. Kayleigh, whom we felt comfortable—not awkward—having in our home many hours each week. (Yes, that meant I didn't have to worry about cleaning or getting out of my pjs before she came over!)

Now my mind turned back to our project. Some days it seemed as if we'd lost many months. Other days I knew we hadn't. God had provided the lessons we needed about not grumbling, not only for this season, but for a lifetime.

We gathered around the dining room table again. I'd always found the dining room table to be the best place to talk about everything concerning this grumble-free challenge. We ate around this table as a family, with John at the head. We talked around this table. We also homeschooled around this table. So when I gathered everyone around it and told them I had something to talk about, they were prepared to listen.

"Are we in trouble?" Maddie asked. It was usually the first thing she asked when I got everyone together. Maybe it was because when the older girls first moved into our home we called family meetings whenever there was a problem or we had to get to the bottom of a situation.

"No, you're not in trouble. I just want to talk about our grumble-free year."

"Are we going to memorize another verse?" one of the little ones called out.

"Do you have something for us to do?" Grace asked.

"Actually, yes." I smiled. "We're going to talk about things we can do without grumbling and arguing."

Maddie raised her eyebrows. "What do you mean?" She glanced at her twin, and worried expressions filled both of their faces.

I softly bit my lip, knowing what I wanted to say but trying to figure out how to explain it. "I've heard it said that many athletes find success by planning ahead for the win. They picture slicing through the water or watching the basketball swish through the net. They plan for victory before it comes, and it seems to me this can work for our non-grumbling too."

"So you want us to think about not grumbling?" Grace's fingers tapped on the tabletop in a steady beat, and I knew she was already done with this conversation before it started. Maybe that came from being fifteen. Or maybe it came from worries over what I would ask them to do.

"Actually, yes." I softly chuckled. "I want us to think ahead through things we normally do in a day and picture ourselves doing them without grumbling. So . . ." I scanned the faces around the table. Some kids looked eager. Others did not. "What is something you can do without grumbling or arguing?"

Alexis, who'd been busily crocheting, piped up from her seat. "I can sing!"

This comment didn't surprise me. Day or night, whenever Alexis was doing anything other than watching television, she was singing. She knew song lyrics better than anyone I'd ever met and could follow a beat. The only problem was she often sang too loudly, especially when she was attempting to sing songs out of her range.

A chorus arose from around the table. "Please don't sing!"

Alexis' jaw dropped, shocked by the response. "But I'm praising the Lord!"

"Yes, we all know you are, but, sweetie, when you're praising God, that's not a time when you usually grumble. Maybe I should have explained myself better. I'm trying to think of a time when you typically grumble . . . then, knowing it's coming up, you think through how you're going to respond instead and do that. Does that make sense?"

I received more nods. "So what could you do without grumbling?" I asked again.

Maddie twirled her long dark hair around her finger. "Go to bed."

"That's a good one. We often have some grumbles there. One of the times we're most likely to grumble is when we're tired."

"When I have to come in for dinner when I want to play," Aly said.

"Yes, that's another time when we grumble . . . when we're disappointed."

"When I do my schoolwork," Grace added.

"Yes."

Anna, the one who quietly sits and takes everything in before commenting, lifted her hand to get my attention. "When we see someone who needs help but we don't want to help."

"That's an awesome one." I wrote it down with the others on the list I'd started to create. "So we see a need and decide to help someone without being asked . . . and do it without grumbling. That would be amazing."

Alexis scoffed. "Don't get your hopes up, Mom."

"Our chores," Maddie commented, again fixing her gaze on her twin.

"Don't look at me like that." Grace puffed up her chest and acted offended. "I don't grumble when I do my chores."

Soft laughter slipped through their lips because we all knew that wasn't the truth—for Grace or for any of us. Including me at times.

"That's a good one, Maddie. But we don't need to point out what other people need to work on. Instead, we need to focus on ourselves. We need to consider what we struggle with and, ahead of time, consider how we could clean, do homework, or go to bed without grumbling."

"We can also think ahead to times when we feel like arguing with you and Dad," Alexis said.

I smiled, happy they were getting it. "Like when?"

Alexis shrugged. "I dunno."

"Like those times when we tell you to turn off the TV, and you know there's only ten minutes left?" I paused. "That's something else I want to talk about. It's not like Dad and I want you to be robots, following our every command. What if your show is almost done? What's a good way you can talk to us about it that's a win for both you and for us?"

Maddie's eyebrows lifted. "Tell you it's almost over? And ask if we can finish."

"Yes, or times when you're told to immediately do your chores and you know your friend will be leaving in a few minutes. You can say something like, 'Can I offer a suggestion?'"

Sissy giggled. "What does that mean?"

"Well, it's a way to tell me you have something to say about this matter. It's not disagreeing or arguing."

Aly shook her head. "That sounds too fancy."

"Okay, you don't have to use those words but maybe something like, 'Mom, I will do what you ask, but my friend has to leave in ten minutes. Can I do my chore in ten minutes?'"

The eyes around the table fixed on mine, and I could see they were considering my words.

"If you have another idea, let me know. All of you are smart. I know you can come up with some good ideas too."

"Like pray about it?" Aly asked.

I chuckled. It reminded me of the Sunday school answer, which is always "Jesus." It seemed that the go-to answer around the Goyer table was "pray about it."

"Yes, we have a secret weapon. When we feel ourselves being rude or ungrateful, we can pray. What can prayer do?"

Buddy's hand shot up in the air, excited that he knew this one. "It can help you be good."

Alexis jumped in next. "It can heal you from grumbling."

"Does God get upset when we ask?" I asked.

A chorus of "No!" rose.

"And remember, like Grandma showed us, we can also praise. Praising is something we can do. It's hard to praise and grumble at the same time."

The kids had sat long enough, and I told them they could go play. I was thankful for the conversation, and I hoped they took to heart that they could come up with ideas too. Even though I took my job of training them seriously, I wanted my children to have an active role in what they were learning. I didn't want my children just blindly following. I hoped the lessons they were learning now would stick. I knew they would benefit them for life.

As Zig Ziglar says, "Be grateful for what you have and stop complaining—it bores everybody else, does you no good, and doesn't solve any problems."[1]

⁓☼⁓

"Being mindful" is a phrase often shared by parenting experts today. Often when people talk about being mindful, it means simply being aware of the present moment. Yet the Bible talked about mindfulness long before it became a popular catchphrase. Romans 12:2 says, "Do not be conformed to this world, but be transformed by the renewal of your mind, that by testing you may discern what is the will of God, what is good and acceptable and perfect" (ESV). Mindfulness then, in the Bible's view, is allowing God to make our minds like his rather than conforming to how the world tells us to think.

In the days following our initial talk, I helped my children work on being mindful—both by being aware of their present moment and also by being thoughtful of possible situations to come and how God would want them to respond. We even did a bit of role-playing.

The sun shone brightly through the dining room windows, and Sissy smiled as she noticed the next-door neighbor heading out to play.

"Mom, can I go ride my bike with my friend?"

The sun felt warm on my shoulders, and I nodded. "Yes, but before we go out, I want to practice something first."

"What?" Sissy crossed her arms and tapped her shoe on the ground. "Can we do it later?"

"It'll just take a minute, but I want to practice something." I glanced at the clock. "Dinner will be ready in forty-five minutes, and I'm going to call you inside. Let's practice me calling you in and you saying, 'Yes, Mom, coming!'"

A sly smile curled up one side of Sissy's mouth. She knew as well as I did that she was prone to grumble when she didn't want to stop playing.

She rushed to the coatrack to get her jacket. "Okay, I'll remember!"

"No, get back here," I called after her. "I want us to do this right. I want you to pause, think through what it will be like to obey, and then I want you to practice saying those words."

Sissy grabbed her jacket and trudged back to me. She squeezed her eyes tight and then opened them.

"Time to come in for dinner," I pretended to call.

"Yes, Mom, I'm coming."

She cocked her head to see if I was satisfied.

I waved her outside. "Good job. Now go have fun."

Sissy rushed out to play, and forty-five minutes later when I called to her, she paused only slightly before answering, "Yes, Mom, I'm coming."

Even her friend seemed surprised by her quick response.

I wish I could say I remembered to use this tool daily, but it was effective when I did remember. It was amazing how well my kids responded when I took the time to walk them through right responses. And I found this tool helped me, too, for doing the same.

Reflection Questions

1. In what ways can thinking ahead about not grumbling help you and your children to achieve success?
2. Often we want our kids to obey immediately without asking questions, but what other ways of communication can you teach that are still respectful?
3. How can role-playing right responses make a difference for our kids, especially role-playing ways to respond without grumbling?

Your Turn

Sit down with your kids and discuss thinking ahead and picturing ways of responding without grumbling. Even better, think of situations when your children are prone to grumble and role-play these situations by having them respond without grumbling and complaining. It may seem strange at first to role-play simple, ordinary parts of their day, but acting out right responses will help kids act right—and respond right—when the time comes.

Chapter 11

HUMILITY WHEN WE MESS UP

We were eight months in, and I was at the point in our journey where I was starting to wonder whether this was a good idea at all. Yes, we'd had some sweet moments and learned some invaluable lessons, but it had been a hard road to walk. We'd try things that would work for a while, and then we'd get busy and forget to focus on the challenge, falling back into old grumbling habits.

John had heard all about my worries and concerns. Sometimes he had that look in his eyes that said, *I told you so.* Other times he tried to talk me down from the "this is hopeless and I simply need to quit" ledge.

Eventually I told John that we needed something to help as a reminder, something that would be with us at all times. So in month eight I purchased something I was certain would work: Grumble-Free bracelets. On one side was imprinted "Grumble-Free," and on the other side, "I can do all things through him."

That was another verse we had all learned together: "I can do all things through [Christ] who strengthens me" (Phil. 4:13 ESV).

The kids were excited about the bracelets—even John and I got one. But the truth is I wondered if I'd bought them just to do something. Or maybe I bought them because I needed the reminder the most. I'd been having huge, grumbly blowups. Mostly on Fridays. It was not pretty.

This had been my worst day for grumbling in a long time. Friday was the end of a long week, and the house was always a disaster. On Thursdays we had therapy all day, followed by me serving at the teen mom support group at night. I usually came home exhausted, got the kids in bed, then collapsed into bed myself. Reality would hit on Friday when all the mess from Thursday (and typically days before that) displayed itself in unrelenting, grubby chaos.

One day frustration rose within me as I surveyed the house.

"Whose shoes are these? Why is leftover food from last night still on the table? And why is there dirty underwear by the back door?"

The children jumped to attention. They rushed around picking up things, and I could see on their faces they didn't want to do anything that would make me more upset. Too bad even their frenzied cleaning didn't work to calm my spirit.

I ranted for at least ten more minutes, pointing out scattered toys and each offending piece of crumbled paper, and then, as if I could see a projection of myself in my mind, the reality of how ugly I was being filled me with shame. I paused and glanced around. By this point my kids were yelling at each other. I'd effectively spread around my bad attitude.

It's Friday . . . learn to deal with Friday. The thought filled my mind, causing me to still my other thoughts.

Friday came after a long week of homeschooling. Friday came after a long day of running and serving. And why did it make me so upset? Because by Friday I was physically weary. Would it be possible to greet Friday, flaws and all, and just accept it? Or maybe even prepare for it—and conquer it without grumbling—as I had previously encouraged my kids to do? It's not as though I didn't understand what triggered me or made me upset.

And that's when the bracelet caught my attention. *I can do all things through him.* That meant Fridays too.

By the time we gathered around the table to start our homeschooling day, my kids were somber. No one wore their typical smiles, and I knew I had to seek forgiveness.

I cleared my throat. "Mommy didn't do a very good job today. My grumbling got out of control. I didn't act nice. I didn't control my tongue. And the Bible talks about this." I opened my Bible to James 3:2 and read, "'Indeed, we all make many mistakes. For if we could control our tongues, we would be perfect and could also control ourselves in every other way'" (NLT).

"The Bible says that?" Grace looked surprised.

"Yes, it does. I didn't do a very good job controlling my tongue this morning. Will you forgive me?"

"Yes, Mom."

"Of course."

"We forgive you," their voices called out.

That was one thing about my kids. When I did mess up and fess up, they were usually quick to forgive.

"I didn't do a good job of controlling my tongue," I continued. "And do you know how hard it is to actually tame it? The Bible talks more about it. Listen to this." I turned back to where I'd been reading.

Indeed, we all make many mistakes. For if we could control our tongues, we would be perfect and could also control ourselves in every other way.

We can make a large horse go wherever we want by means of a small bit in its mouth. And a small rudder makes a huge ship turn wherever the pilot chooses to go, even though the winds are strong. In the same way, the tongue is a small thing that makes grand speeches.

But a tiny spark can set a great forest on fire. And among all the parts of the body, the tongue is a flame of fire. It is a whole world of wickedness, corrupting your entire body. It can set your whole life on fire, for it is set on fire by hell itself.

People can tame all kinds of animals, birds, reptiles, and fish, but no one can tame the tongue. It is restless and evil, full of deadly poison. Sometimes it praises our Lord and Father, and sometimes it curses those who have been made in the image of God. And so blessing and cursing come pouring out of the same mouth. Surely, my brothers and sisters, this is not right! (NLT)

I paused and lifted my head. "That's James 3:2–10."

"No way!" Fifteen-year-old Maddie's jaw dropped toward her chest. "The Bible really says that? I don't believe it." She extended her hand, motioning me to put my Bible into it. I did. She found the passage and her eyes grew wider. "Wow, it really does say that."

"Yes, and what do you think all that means?"

"Our tongues are hard to control?" Ten-year-old Sissy posed it like a question.

"That's right. Good job listening."

"If you don't watch what you're saying, you can end up in the middle of troubles," Maddie said.

"None of us can control our tongues completely, except maybe mute people who can't talk," Grace commented.

"That's true . . . but I'm sure they could find ways to grumble, couldn't they?"

Seventeen-year-old Anna brushed her long hair back from her face. "I like the part that says that blessing and cursing come from the same mouth, and that isn't right."

"It isn't right. And I know I've been doing a lot of grumbling this morning. How can we fix that? What can we do instead?"

"Oh, oh!" Thirteen-year-old Alexis jumped up from her chair, raising her hand. "We could each write something we are thankful for and put it into the Gratitude Jar."

"Can we do it now?" Maddie asked, her face brightening.

"I can get the stuff!" Alexis jumped up, grabbed the jar, paper, and pens, and passed them out.

"Good idea . . ." I could barely get the words out of my mouth before everyone started writing.

"We're supposed to write something we're thankful for?" Sissy posed another question.

"Yes, we're choosing to praise, not grumble," Maddie commented. Then she turned to her two youngest siblings, Aly and Buddy. "Let me know if you need help spelling any words."

Alexis placed the Gratitude Jar in front of me. I'd nearly given up on it after realizing that I couldn't force thankfulness. The sole papers inside were still the nine tightly folded squares Alexis had begrudgingly put inside the jar months ago. I looked around the table at the smiles. No one was begrudgingly doing it now. They all excitedly wrote down things they were thankful for. What a difference from just thirty minutes ago.

"Can we do more than one?" Grace asked.

"Sure, as many as you like." I smiled. "And while you're at it, there's a verse I'm going to find. One I think you'll all like."

I turned my Bible to Psalm 136. I had come across these verses recently, and I knew I wanted to share them with the kids. Now, it seemed, was the perfect time.

Once everyone had finished writing their notes for the jar, they turned their attention back to me.

"When we're grumbling, what are we not doing?" I asked.

"Praising!" they all said at once.

"Well, now we're going to praise together. I'm going to read a few lines of this verse, and you tell me what you notice." Then I read Psalm 136:1–3 to them.

> Give thanks to the LORD, for he is good.
> *His love endures forever.*
> Give thanks to the God of gods.
> *His love endures forever.*
> Give thanks to the Lord of lords:
> *His love endures forever.*

Alexis waved her hand. "Oh, after each part it says, 'His love endures forever.'"

"Yes, exactly. And it does that through the whole chapter—all twenty-six verses. So I'm going to read the first part aloud, and you all say the second part aloud. Got it?"

They all nodded, and I began. I read through the whole psalm, and after each verse they said, "His love endures forever." As we continued my heart swelled with joy. Tears rimmed my eyes to hear my children praising God in unison, and I began to wonder why I hadn't done this more often. I also wondered why I had let Fridays take such a hold of me.

It was amazing, really, what could happen when I was willing to humble myself, explain how hard it was to control one's tongue, and then encourage my kids to turn to praise instead. It didn't just change the moment. It changed the day.

I looked down to my bracelet again. *Yes, I can do all things through him who strengthens me.*

Reflection Questions

1. What are your "Fridays"—the days or events that make it most challenging to hold your tongue?
2. What happens when you are willing to humble yourself and confess when grumbles take over?
3. How can you fill your mind full of praise—instead of grumbles—today?

Your Turn

One of my favorite Bible stories is that of Zacchaeus. The story is in Luke 19:1–10, and it's worth reading. It starts when Jesus entered Jericho and crowds pressed in, yet out of everyone Zacchaeus is specifically mentioned. And he's described three ways: as a chief tax collector, wealthy, and short. Zacchaeus wanted to see Jesus so much that he humbled himself and climbed a sycamore fig tree. Jesus spotted him, and soon Zacchaeus had a visitor for lunch. Again, Zacchaeus's humility was on display because, without prompting, he offered to give half of his possessions to the poor and pay back anyone he'd cheated four times the amount. While the crowds had pressed in to see what Jesus could do for them, Zacchaeus humbled himself, knowing he needed to change. That's what humility does: it causes us to take a closer look at ourselves.

We may understand that we need to change before we can guide our kids to make better choices, but the one thing that truly makes change happen is humility. Yet it's also a hard pill to swallow. It's stripping off our smugness that declares, "I have my act together," to reveal our flaws.

And just as Jesus spotted Zacchaeus and visited him, Jesus comes to us too. There are many who want Jesus for what they can get from him, but change only comes when our humility shows Jesus we're ready to give up what we hold most closely: our right to ourselves.

My kids noted my humility, and they were quick to forgive. More than that, they were quick to praise. Humility reminds everyone where true change comes from and turns our hearts to giving glory to the God who's given so much to us.

Think about a time when you were wrong about something when it came to your kids. Did you humble yourself and own up to it?

When you do fail—because we all do at some point—be quick to seek forgiveness from your kids. First, it's a good model for our kids to follow. Second, it helps restore hurts. And third, it invites Jesus into the moment. Our humility points to him.

Chapter 12

LOST IN THE MIDDLE OF INGRATITUDE

One weekend my whole family traveled with me on a speaking trip to a homeschool conference. John drove and helped at the book table. I spoke. The kids attended workshops for their age groups, covered every inch of the exhibit hall, and made new friends.

After packing up all our things, we arrived back at home after midnight. We let the kids sleep in the following day, a Sunday, but that meant we missed church. Once we did get up and moving, we had a full house—grown kids and grandkids in addition to our regular household of eleven. It was great but exhausting. And as I looked ahead to the week to come, I knew things would be getting harder, not easier.

Weary from the previous week, I woke up early Monday morning because my grandma was having back surgery. It turned out her back hadn't healed as the doctor had hoped. Even though we were diligent about putting on her back brace whenever she sat up or stood, the break had gotten worse. Because of her age and osteoporosis, the doctor didn't believe her back would heal on its own. Thus the surgery.

It was hard seeing her wheeled away, but a few hours later we received a good report. The surgery had gone well. Now she was back in the hospital room recovering, which meant I was trying to spend as much time up there as I could. Yet that didn't mean things were slowing down at home.

Monday was also Anna's eighteenth birthday, and we were planning to have a houseful of people that night, but I was so weary already that a celebration simply seemed like work, not fun. Add on a teen's rebellion from the previous evening, an attitude I still had to deal with. The day was a heavy, busy one. Yet maybe that's only because I was looking at my day with the wrong perspective.

The truth was, I had so much to be thankful about. The previous week a family friend had sold us a car for much less than its value, and now my daughter would have a car for college. My mother had arrived recently to help with my grandmother. And let's not forget that my grandmother's surgery went well, even though she was eighty-eight years old.

It was so easy to get caught up in everything that needed to be fixed and done, but truthfully the root of my angst was my grumbling heart. I loved my big family, but inside I grumbled because I didn't have time for myself.

I loved traveling to speak, but I grumbled because it was so much work, especially taking my family along.

I was very grateful to be in my forties and still have my grandmother around, but my heart already carried heaviness as I realized what the weeks ahead were going to look like as I cared for her after surgery.

I was also so quick to figure out the right consequences for my wayward teen that I didn't pause to realize that her attitude and actions were a red flag, alerting me that there was a connection that needed to be made. What looked like outright rebellion was really a green light to connect with her, to seek her heart.

As I took time to confess my grumbling heart and sought to lift it instead to God, my attitude began to change. Today was a day of celebration. My daughter was eighteen, and God had given us the opportunity to love her and parent her for three years and to do our best to guide her into adulthood. She was a beautiful young lady who loved God and was making good decisions—we needed to celebrate that!

Today was also a day of celebration because I still had my grandmother and family filled my life. As my husband, John, always says, "There's a whole lot of living going on here."

As I thought about all that was happening, I realized that in the midst of it all was God. This life we'd been living had all started with me saying, *God, I'll do anything for you. Anything.* While it seemed like a noble thought then, the reality was that following Jesus was a whole lot of work day by day. It reminded me of Jesus' conversation with Peter on the night before his death in John 13:36–38:

> Simon Peter asked him, "Lord, where are you going?"
>
> Jesus replied, "Where I am going, you cannot follow now, but you will follow later."
>
> Peter asked, "Lord, why can't I follow you now? I will lay down my life for you."
>
> Then Jesus answered, "Will you really lay down your life

for me? Very truly I tell you, before the rooster crows, you will disown me three times!"

Oh, Peter, you had no clue what you were saying, did you? Like me, you had all the right intentions, but you had no idea what your declaration would mean or where it would take you. You had no idea of the tears that would be shed, the conflict you'd face, and the opposition that would come.

As Oswald Chambers said:

It is much easier to die than to lay down your life day in and day out with the sense of the high calling of God. We are not made for the bright-shining moments of life, but we have to walk in the light of them in our everyday ways. . . . If I am a friend of Jesus, I must deliberately and carefully lay down my life for him. It is a difficult thing to do, and thank God that it is.[1]

If laying down my life were easy, then I wouldn't need Jesus. I wouldn't need to get up early, seek his face, and ask him to transform my grumbling heart even before the day begins.

Peter's life was transformed as he faced hardship, and Peter's heart was transformed too. Later, the man who was ready to fight and die for Jesus realized it wasn't one grand display that would prove his love but the daily pouring out.

In a letter to fellow believers, Peter wrote, "Above all, love each other deeply, because love covers over a multitude of sins. Offer hospitality to one another without grumbling. Each of you should use whatever gift you have received to serve others, as faithful stewards of God's grace in its various forms" (1 Peter 4:8–10).

That day I awoke with a grumbling heart, but as I sat before

God everything changed—not externally but internally. And I knew that my day—as busy as it was—would be transformed too.

Getting lost in the middle of ingratitude happened so easily, but refocusing—that was the harder part. How much easier life would be if we could just be brave and do one grand gesture for God and then everything would be smooth from there. Instead, life means laying down oneself over and over again—for your grandmother, for your new-to-adulthood child, and for your difficult teen.

That's what following Jesus truly is all about. Loving through the hardships and when we feel weary. Choosing to praise instead of grumble, and pausing to find God in the midst of busyness.

Maybe soon I'd be able to take a moment to rest . . . but now it was time to step out and love, serve, and praise.

Reflection Questions

1. When was the last time you found yourself in the middle of ingratitude?
2. Even though busy lives filled with challenges can make us weary, how does seeking God and praising him in the midst of it change things?
3. What is something you grumbled about today that you can find a way to thank God for instead?

Your Turn

Sometimes we think bravery is doing something big for God, but my friend Holley Gerth says, "Simply doing the next thing is often the bravest choice we can make." I'll dare to add to that. Simply doing the next thing (without grumbling) is often the bravest choice we can make.

What do you face today? What is on your to-do list? If you don't have a list, make one. And then after each item add: *without grumbling*.

Chapter 13

PRAYER MAKES A DIFFERENCE

When I started on this journey, I saw grumbling as something I needed to fix. I'd lie in bed with John and think about ideas. We'd talk about our grumbling ways and think through things we could do to try to help.

While John was more realistic, I imagined that if I could come up with the perfect strategy and on-target activities we could nail this grumbling for good. I thought it was something I needed to control and that it needed to happen now. Then life got in the way.

Lost childcare, shrinking work hours, months of sickness. Plus Grandma. And in the midst of that was my daughter's senior year, which meant there were college visits, schedules, transcripts, and scholarships to manage. I did what I could to work on the grumble-free project, but in the back of my mind I felt it wasn't enough.

Yet maybe God knew this was the right year to tackle it all. Maybe he knew I needed to be slowed down from my "fixing" to take the whole thing in a slower, more natural way.

What we'd accomplished so far:

- All of us agreed grumbling was something we needed to work on.
- All of us realized that grumbling comes in many forms, and we all were now aware of our various forms.
- All of us understood better how much God hates grumbling.
- All of us were now quick to notice it and see it as a problem. (Of course my kids were quickest to point out when their brother or sister was having a grumbling problem.)
- We now talked about grumbling often and had come up with skills to help ourselves do better.
- We'd memorized scriptures together.
- We'd turned to God for help.
- We'd come to understand that the opposite of grumbling was thankfulness, and when we grumbled we were saying more about how much we trusted God than anything else.

Yes, we were well over halfway through the year, and, yes, I hadn't done many of the projects I had planned, but things were changing. We were more aware. Our hearts had softened. Our minds had opened. Our lips were speaking thanksgiving more than grumbling. What a success!

Maybe this was the right track. We were seeing how God's Word really did apply to every part of our lives. We understood how grumbling and thanksgiving truly impacted every part of us.

The week after Grandma's surgery, we started our Monday with a new kind of thanksgiving, and it came by way of prayer journals. I wish I could say this was something I'd planned when

I first considered our grumble-free year, but it wasn't. Instead, I'd realized when I was sitting in the hospital room with my grandma that it was only a few days until Easter and I hadn't yet purchased anything for my kids.

In our house, Easter gifts have nothing to do with Easter bunnies. Instead, I've tried to find something that will help my kids grow spiritually. Sometimes I've given Christian music CDs or DVDs. Other Easters I've given Bibles or devotional books. And this year, as I considered how much prayer had helped us on our grumble-free journey, I thought of prayer journals. So I ordered them for my kids.

That morning, as we all gathered around the dining room table for prayer and Bible reading, my little kids pulled out their journals since theirs had actually arrived on time. The first line asked them to write something about their day. The second line had them write something they were thankful for, and the third line had a place where they could write a request. The kids loved having a place to record their thoughts, and I did too. I had to laugh when seven-year-old Buddy wrote down he was thankful for canned spaghetti.

The words my little kids wrote in their thankful spot became part of their spoken prayer. Now they could start each day with a thankful heart, even if it was simply the canned spaghetti that my son was thankful for.

I was still waiting for the older girls' prayer journals to come in. The younger kids had found so much joy in them; I knew the older girls would too. As I'd been learning, things didn't always work on my time schedule, yet God's timing was perfect. I'd wanted to approach this grumble-free year with lists to check off, but God showed me what it meant to slow down, to look to him, and to connect with my kids over whatever the days held.

I shudder now thinking of what would have happened if I'd

had the opportunity to push my kids harder. When I first considered what a grumble-free year would look like, I'd focused on the huge leap that needed to happen to get us from where we were to where we needed to be. I'd thought each month would mean me being on top of all aspects of my plan, but my pushiness usually made things worse, not better—as witnessed by my conflict with Alexis over the Gratitude Jar.

I'm so thankful I was forced to slow down and to let the plan come from our circumstances and not my ideas. There were many times we talked about grumbling in ways I hadn't devised. And maybe it would be one of those conversations that ended up helping my kids the most in their lives.

Maybe one of those conversations that placed a seed of truth in my kids' hearts was helping them even now. Maybe their growing gratitude was already making a difference.

※

When we started our grumble-free year, I thought the pages of this book would be filled with what we'd start doing in the year. What I didn't realize was that one of the areas where it would have the greatest impact on my kids was something they'd already been doing for a while.

Twice in the past week I'd had people I didn't know well praise my kids—how they were serving others, how they were playing with younger kids, and how positive their attitudes were. In all of these cases, my kids were serving others and volunteering.

For so long service had been a part of our lives, but it wasn't something I'd grown up with. My personal volunteering started after reading verses like Isaiah 1:17: "Learn to do right; seek justice.

Defend the oppressed. Take up the cause of the fatherless; plead the case of the widow." And so I volunteered in church, starting with the nursery. Around the same time I felt the call to ask my grandparents to move in with us. God also spoke to my heart about helping to start a crisis pregnancy center, and I "dragged" my three oldest kids along to help. I was still helping, and every week I led a teen mom support group in our church.

I knew service helped others, but through the years—and even more so through writing this book—I'd come to realize it had also helped my kids. Service had trained my children to look beyond themselves. They saw needs, they cared, and they gave.

As my kids saw the needs of others, they realized how much they had themselves. It's hard to complain about having nothing to wear when earlier that week they'd helped a teen mom by providing clothes and diapers for her baby. My best may not be the best, but if I'm doing my best to love and serve others—and inviting my kids to do the same—it will make a difference.

In his book *Quiet Talks on Prayer*, S. D. Gordon said, "For if a man is to pray right, he must first *be* right in his motives and life. And if a man *be* right, and put the practice of praying in its right place, then his serving and giving and speaking will be fairly fragrant with the presence of God."[1]

It was important for me to give my kids prayer journals to help them better their prayer lives and gain a more thankful perspective. But maybe another way of going about this was something we'd already been doing: serving. For as they served they learned to see through eyes of gratitude and better understood how to pray, what to pray, and whom to pray for.

And also, in their service, someone else might see something special and decide they wanted to be a part of it too.

※

Arriving at the teen mom support group that I led, the older girls and I jumped into action. I busily began setting up the tables while also greeting the teen moms who showed up early. Anna, Maddie, and Grace set out the baby clothes, which were available for the moms to shop (for free). We all ate dinner together, and then, while I facilitated the support group meeting, my teens—along with adult helpers—babysat.

It seemed like an ordinary evening, but when the girls got back in the car they had an amazing story to tell me. They began sharing about a conversation they'd had with one of the adult volunteers, Liz. Liz was also a member of our church.

"Mom, we told her how great it was to be adopted and how hard it was in foster care," Maddie said. "We told her how amazing you and Dad are for adopting us. I mean, you could have totally been empty nesters right now, going on vacations and stuff, and instead you're still taking care of all these kids."

I listened as the teens took turns sharing about all they told Liz.

"We told her what it had been like in foster care. What it was like being separated. We told her about our failed adoption," Grace said.

"And I told her how we prayed for a mom and dad . . . someone who would keep us together," Maddie added.

Tears filled my eyes. My heart filled with joy over their gratitude. So many times I found it easy to focus on all the challenges, but as I listened to my daughters speak, I was reminded of all the joys. Their lives—my life—had been forever changed, and they were quick to tell someone that.

"Liz was so amazed, Mom," Maddie added. "She told us that we are blessed to have our family. And you know what I told her . . ." Maddie's voice trailed off.

"What was that? I'm almost afraid to ask."

"I told her she needed to adopt some kids too. Her last kid just went to college. She's just like you were."

I chuckled. "And what did Liz say about that?"

"She said she'd think about it." A smile filled Grace's face. "And do you know what else we told her? We told her we were going to pray that she and her husband would say yes!"

Weeks passed, and I forgot about the conversation . . . until I saw Liz at church. We greeted each other in the foyer, and then Liz placed a hand on her hip.

"So," she said with a smirk. "Your girls really think you're amazing."

I chuckled. "Oh, yes, I heard you had quite the conversation with them a few weeks ago. That's good they told you how thankful they were and not all the dirt."

"Yes, well, they went on and on about how great you both are. But that's not all." Liz cocked her head. "Do you know what they told me? They said, 'Why don't you adopt kids, Liz? You don't have an excuse.'"

"Oh no." I covered my mouth with my hand. "I'm so sorry."

"Oh, don't be sorry." She gripped my hand and gave it a squeeze. "I needed to hear that. Those words didn't leave my mind. 'What about you?' I even talked to my husband about it, and we've been praying. And you know what? They're right. We have no excuse. We've already signed up for the training. We're going to do it. We're going to try to adopt some older kids too."

Joy filled me. I squealed and gave Liz a hug. The girls had been praying about this, I had no doubt. And now . . . well, I couldn't wait to see what God was going to do. Lives would be forever changed because my teens had shared their gratitude.

Prayer changed things. Thankfulness changed things, and sharing our stories did too. I couldn't wait to tell the girls.

Reflection Questions

1. Why is it important to pause and see how far we've come, even when we feel as if we have a long way to go?
2. How does serving others change what we pray for and how we see our lives? How does it sometimes make us more grateful?
3. How has another person's personal story of gratitude made you look at your life differently?

Your Turn

Start by creating prayer journals for you and your kids. Take time to write in them daily. Jot down your needs, your requests, and what you're thankful for. This daily habit will go a long way in transforming hearts.

Also, consider ways you can serve in your church and your community as a family. As your family gives to others, you'll be more aware of the needs of those around you. Looking at what others have and don't have can help your kids look at their own lives with more gratefulness, and soon that gratefulness might just spill out in unexpected ways.

Chapter 14

HEART MESSES

For the last few months we'd been reading through *The Whole Bible Story* by Dr. William H. Marty. It's a book that tells everything that happened in the Bible in plain English. I enjoyed reading this with my kids. It took us on a journey through Scripture with the very sinful, grumbling people of the Bible.

The Israelites in the desert offered a clear display of what happens when we become dissatisfied with what God provides and, in a sense, dissatisfied with God. In my personal quiet time I'd been reading through Psalm 106, and I decided to read it aloud to my kids.

> They forgot the God who saved them,
> who had done great things in Egypt,
> miracles in the land of Ham
> and awesome deeds by the Red Sea.
> So he said he would destroy them—
> had not Moses, his chosen one,
> stood in the breach before him

to keep his wrath from destroying them.
Then they despised the pleasant land;
they did not believe his promise.
They grumbled in their tents
and did not obey the LORD. (Ps. 106:21–25)

"The whole problem starts with the first part," I explained to my kids. "'They forgot the God who saved them.' That's the root of grumbling. We forget about God."

The kids nodded. Some colored as they listened. Some played with Perler beads. My kids did a better job of listening—interacting—when they were doing something with their hands.

We continued to talk about others who forgot about God, mostly the kings of Israel. After David, there were a few good kings: Hezekiah and Josiah, to name two. But for the most part, all the kings forgot God and worshiped idols.

Over the last few months, as I'd read about the kings' wicked ways, my kids had moaned, "Why won't they ever learn?"

"Why don't we ever learn?" I asked. "We think about ourselves, and we forget about God just like they did."

"And then we grumble," Maddie added.

"Yes, and then we grumble," I confirmed.

But it wasn't enough to just teach my kids about those who did the wrong thing. I also called out those who did what's right.

One of the best talks we had was about Shadrach, Meshach, and Abednego.

"They were taken as exiles and served a pagan king, yet they didn't forget God. Not only that, but they believed he would save them from the fire—and if he didn't, they claimed God was still worth dying for. There was no grumbling on their lips, even as they stepped toward that blazing fire," I explained. "They didn't forget God, and God didn't forget them. He was with them in their mess."

I paused and thought about our homeschooling year. When we started in August, I'd had no idea of the fire to come. In fact, I thought I'd fully done everything I could to prepare.

More than any other homeschooling year, I'd organized every part of the plan ahead of time. I'd prearranged each week's assignments. I'd even taken apart my kids' workbooks and sorted the sheets into folders by the week they would need them.

I'd organized my schedule and planned my teaching blocks of time and my working blocks of time. And more than any other year, I'd set emotional and spiritual goals through this grumble-free challenge.

Even so, I had no idea what was to come. Nothing could have prepared me for it. And while my early planning helped me in some ways (at least I knew what homework assignments my kids were to do next), I couldn't have foreseen the manner in which God would change our hearts.

I thought our success would have come from the very scheduled and organized year I had mapped out, but it was through the really hard stuff—the heartbreaking stuff—that my family found Jesus. We discovered him with us in the fire.

Then, as we studied the Scriptures—especially the Old Testament—one thing became vividly clear: the Israelites grumbled and complained *a lot*. They did so collectively and individually. It's as if they didn't have a faithful bone in their bodies; every sentence they spoke a complaint.

"Seriously, they're complaining again?" Alexis declared in exasperation as I read.

"Hello, people. What about what God's already done?" Grace lamented. "Aren't you going to remember that?"

"These people are dumb," Sissy announced, tossing her bangs out of her face like she always did when she was frustrated.

"Yeah, dumb!" Buddy added, pounding his fists on the table. He often copied Sissy but added his own little boy growl as he did.

"They are us." My eyes scanned the dining room table. Beads, sewing supplies, and colored pencils—all the things my kids had gotten out to keep them occupied as I read—covered the surface.

"It's us all the time. We don't like how we are treated. We think someone else has an easier time. Or they have something we don't. We don't like our lips and want to have Kylie Jenner's lips. We stand in the closet and mumble that we don't have anything to wear."

Grace smirked at me. "Gee, Mom, throw us under the bus."

"It's true." Maddie pushed her glasses up on her nose and then crossed her arms over her chest. "We do grumble a lot. Sometimes we try hard, but a lot of times we still don't."

"I don't always grumble," commented Alexis, and everyone laughed.

"Um, remember just last night when I reminded you to go clean your room?"

She offered a knowing smile and rolled her eyes as only a thirteen-year-old girl can. "Well . . . that's because . . ."

I held up my hand, cutting off her words. "I know, I know—just a one-time occurrence," I conceded, even though we both knew it wasn't. It was something that needed to be fixed too.

While reading through *The Whole Bible Story*, it was clear the Israelites struggled with their grumbling because they refused to tackle the messes they created. They refused to ditch the idols, and they were always looking to what other nations had, thinking they had it better. The root of their grumbling came down to the condition of their hearts—and the condition of their lives. This hit close to home, and it was time our family took care of a few messes we continually grumbled about but refused to change.

Over the last few weeks, Alexis had been spending a lot of time in her room, days actually, attempting to clean it. But she never got very far. She had too much stuff for such a little space—one-third of a room that she shared with her sisters. It was time to make a change.

Nathan moving out made a new bedroom situation possible. Now eighteen, Anna got to move out of the walk-through room into Nathan's old room, and Alexis got to move into Anna's space because it was her stuff that seemed to spill out of her corner of the room and invade her sisters' spaces.

"Mom, can you tell Alexis to clean up her stuff? It's on my side of the room." The complaints were endless.

I often told myself, *So much for the Grumble-Free Year. We are getting* nowhere. Especially with all the grumbles about bedroom messes going on.

Thankfully, now we had a solution: Alexis had her own space.

Anna moved into Nathan's room, but Alexis had to wait to move because my mom was still staying with us and she was in Anna's room. Another challenging thing about the move was that Alexis is a pack rat. She keeps everything—from old chip bags to free pencils given out at doctors' offices to scraps of old newspapers. Since Alexis had been moved so many times in foster care and had lost so many things, it's almost as if she refuses to give up anything that belongs to her, ever.

Even though they were eager to have one less person in their room, I warned her sisters, "Don't be in such a hurry to move all her stuff out at once. Let's take it slowly. I want to help Alexis go through her things and get rid of the stuff she doesn't need."

Those words only held the twins back a few days. Days later, as soon as I came home from a therapy appointment with some of the kids, Alexis rushed to me. "Mom, they took everything of mine and just dumped it in the middle of the floor. I can't even walk in there now!"

Now that Alexis could move in and the girls' rooms were in disarray, I gave them the assignment of getting their bedrooms in order, but then the weather turned warm and drew them outside and they were doing anything but that. I found myself grumbling. Of course they were grumbling, too, whenever they came back inside. No one was happy with the mess.

We needed to fix this.

And that's when I came up with an ultimatum for the entire family: "No one can have electronics, watch TV, or go outside until your room is clean. You need to clean it well—get rid of stuff, put everything in its place, and then you have to keep it clean. It won't be that hard to maintain if you do it on a daily basis." (And as I heard my words, I could almost hear God's numerous warnings to the Israelites running through my head.)

I expected to get a lot of pushback, but it didn't happen. It was almost as if it was a relief. The kids were being forced to deal with messes they didn't enjoy.

The older girls launched into their rooms, and I jumped in to help the little kids. For me and the three younger ones, it took five hours, resulting in three bags of garbage and three more bags of stuff to give away. For the twins and Alexis, it took three days.

"Back up in your room until it is done. Find every piece of trash and cast it away . . ." (Was that being a little too dramatic?)

In the end, their "done" wasn't quite my "done," but I was still impressed! Their rooms were by far cleaner and more organized than I had seen them since the day they all moved in.

It took another thirty minutes for them to finish the last of the things I pointed out, but it was such a good feeling to see everything neat and in its place. The girls seemed even more excited than I was. They knew where all their stuff was. They had gotten rid of worthless junk, and they liked the sense of accomplishment.

I realized then how many *years* we'd fallen into the same trap of grumbling, complaining, and putting up with the mess when all we needed to do was fix it. At least once a day I'd grumbled about their messy rooms. Just think of all that grumbling we could have saved if I'd just given the ultimatum sooner.

Not that I had any expectations that the kids would be able to keep their rooms perfectly clean. If God couldn't keep the Israelites from going back to their junk, I knew I wasn't going to be able to keep the kids from going back to theirs. But at least we had a starting point.

·⬦·

In the Bible the Israelites often grumbled because their bad choices led them to horrible messes. In our case, like with bedrooms, grumbling became a habit because we all got into a rut. My girls didn't want to take time to clean up their messes, so they simply grumbled about each other's messes. I didn't want to have to be firm, put my foot down, and give an ultimatum. So I let it slide. But that just led to my grumbling mixing in with theirs. "You are just so messy . . . you really need to clean up your stuff!"

Thankfully, God has always known that letting people live in their messes doesn't benefit them. He sent prophets time and time again to tell both kings and their subjects alike to get their act together. And ultimately he sent his Son to save us from our messes and to model a better way of living going forward.

Grumbling directly or indirectly expresses that God has not provided what we think we need. We look at our messes, and instead of accepting that at least some of the blame falls on us, our complaining says, "He is not good, wise, loving, or faithful." After all, if we truly believed he was all of these things, we would complain a lot less. And the truth is that God has provided everything we need. He's given us himself. He's given Jesus—God in flesh—to show us how to truly live. To get us out of our messes.

We have seen in the Bible, as we have seen when it comes to girls' bedrooms, that it doesn't help anything simply to grumble about the messes that inevitably come in our lives. We have to deal with our messes, and thankfully, because of Jesus, we don't have to deal with our heart messes alone.

Reflection Questions

1. What is a mess you've had to walk through in everyday life? Did you do it with grumbling or with faith in God?
2. How is it easy to notice the grumbling and lack of faith of people in the Bible, but it's harder to see it in ourselves?
3. How can focusing on how Jesus lived help you with your own attitude and grumbling? Is there a mess you need to clean up with God's help?

Your Turn

Sometimes it takes us getting tired of the grumbling to pause and look at the messes. And sometimes it takes us rolling up our sleeves and tackling the messes to get the grumbling to stop.

Think of something in your life that you've been grumbling about. Is there a mess you need to tackle? It's easy to forget that God is there to help us get out of our messes. Maybe he will do this by providing strength, motivation, or help. Set a time to tackle that big project and feel the relief on the other side.

Chapter 15

FOR THE FAME

As I mentioned before, John and I have a daughter who, more than anything, wants to be famous. As someone who was in foster care at a very young age, was separated often from her sisters, and got moved from place to place with no control, Alexis wants to be seen, known, appreciated, and to have control—something she believes she's sure to find in Hollywood.

Almost daily she talks about me helping her pursue her dream of becoming a movie star, yet this is the same daughter who struggles the most with talking back and grumbling. It's a continual problem, and even as I witnessed grumble-free attitudes working throughout our home, it seemed that nothing we'd said or done had managed to influence this thirteen-year-old for the better. Well, except for yesterday.

We only had three weeks left of homeschool, and I'd been on a wild streak about getting everything wrapped up and sorted for this year and prepared for the next year. But there was quite a lot to put away and organize. In addition to the world map taped to my china cabinet, my buffet table was filled with schoolbooks. I also had milk crates filled with files of lesson plans and two rolling crates of school supplies. Our dining room is a room we do life in—both schooling and gathering as a family for dinner. It is far from Pinterest perfect, but I like to keep it neat, and Alexis is my go-to person to help me keep it organized.

I asked her yesterday to help me sort our bins of colored pencils, crayons, and markers, which led to an interesting conversation.

"Mom, someday I want to be famous. I want it more than anything."

"I know." I sighed, imagining the same conversation playing out where she begs me to take her to Los Angeles so she can audition and me telling her she's going to have to pursue that dream when she's eighteen years old because my priority as a mom is to raise her up to know and love Jesus, not for her to become a child star. But before I launched into my typical shooting-down-her-dreams-for-reality talk, I remembered something I'd heard on a recent podcast.

"You know," I told her. "If you want to get in Hollywood later, it's important to start working on the little stuff now."

"What do you mean?"

"Well, why do you want to get to Hollywood? Why do you want to be famous? Do you want people to think you're wonderful and sing their praises to you?" I specifically worded my questions this way. I knew she'd pick up on the word *praises*. She's very insightful like that.

Alexis' brow furrowed. She paused her sorting of markers, formulating an answer in her head. "Well, if I were famous, every time before I sang or acted, I'd tell people about Jesus and how I'm using the gifts and talents he gave me."

I smiled and nodded. "Yes, that would be a good thing to

do—share the good news of Jesus like that—and it would reach a lot of people, but are you doing that now . . . right where you are?"

At my words the furrows in my daughter's brow deepened. Her shoulders squared, and her jaw jutted out. I could feel her defenses rising—reality hitting the hazy, bedazzled fantasy in her mind.

"Well, I can't share Jesus now because everyone who lives by us is already a Christian." Her words came out in a huff. This isn't completely true, but I decided not to argue that point.

"Well, I'm not talking about just telling people about Jesus, although that's important. I'm talking about living a life that displays the fruit of the Spirit—love, joy, peace, patience, kindness, goodness, faithfulness, gentleness, and self-control. Those things in our lives are evidence of Jesus, and people can see it no matter what we're doing, no matter where we are."

"Well, I'm trying!" Her voice had a quiver to it, and she crossed her arms over her chest.

I leaned in toward her and softened my voice. I didn't want to crush her spirit, but for the past weeks and months I'd been so busy trying to control her actions and get her not to grumble with no success. Now I had a feeling we were finally getting to the heart of the matter.

"I know you do try, sweetie, but do you remember what we talked about this morning in Bible study? Do you remember how we become loving, joyful, peaceful, and self-controlled? Does it come from trying harder?"

"No, it comes from God's Spirit in us."

"Yes, and the fruit will come when we ask for more help from Jesus, not depending on ourselves. There's something else important too. Luke 16:10 says, 'Whoever can be trusted with very little, can also be trusted with much.' If you want to live a life as a famous person who displays God in all you do, you need to start doing that in your life today—in your home—right now with the people around you. God's not going to give you influence over millions of people if you aren't doing a good job at loving the ten other people who live right around you."

Alexis continued sorting pencils and markers as she thought about this a minute. "So are you saying that if I love my brothers and sisters, God will make me famous?"

I held back a chuckle. "I'm saying that if you can be trusted with the little you have, God will give you more. Just like if I gave you $100 to start a business. If I came back a month later and you had used that money just to buy candy and toys for yourself and your friends, do you think I would give you more money to continue your business?"

"No."

"Right, but if you were using what I gave you in a good way, I'd give you more because I'd see you were being responsible. So, in the same way, if you really care for the people around you—speaking to them with love and consideration without grumbling—God will most likely give you more people to care for. He wouldn't want to give you lots of fans if you can't even be nice to the people in your own house."

She seemed to be taking it in, so I continued.

"You know, I was just listening to a podcast where a CEO— which is the head boss—of a company was talking about giving people small jobs to see how they handled them before she gave them big jobs. She said, 'If someone can't get my coffee order right, I'm not going to trust them with the details of a million-dollar client.' And that's what I'm talking about here. If you can't get this right—the relationships in our home and your attitude—I have a feeling God's not going to give you a stage."

I paused again, and I could see that somehow, out of everything I'd said, this was making sense to her. I reached over tenderly and gave her hand a squeeze.

"So I'd really just encourage you to turn to Jesus and ask him to help you on the inside so that you can treat people better on the outside, and this includes not grumbling."

She nodded, and the conversation moved on from there, but I could tell she was really working on her attitude the rest of the night. Instead of complaining about someone else getting to pick the television show, she encouragingly gave them ideas of what they could pick. She was thoughtful with her responses to others, and more than once John and I remarked on her positive attitude, causing her to smile.

As I laid my head on my pillow that night, thankfulness filled my heart. I never could have planned or orchestrated that conversation if I'd tried, yet being present with my daughter and open to the Spirit of God stirring within me had brought about something we both needed: a way to consider God's glory in the midst of our grumble-free attempts.

I needed to hear the very words I had spoken to my daughter. Truth be told, deep down I'd hoped this grumble-free journey would succeed so others might get a glimpse of what an insightful and resourceful mom I was. Yet if there was anything I'd discovered, it was this: my deepening dependence on God—and on his Spirit within—was the greater good coming out of my attempts at learning to be grumble-free.

When we started the Grumble-Free Year, there was a lot going on in my life.

In those early days, I would have told you that all of the everyday things of life were more than enough to handle, much less adding the weight of tackling such a big project. And yet I expected the coming days to be similar to those I typically faced: hard but doable.

If God would have given me a glimpse of what was to come, there's no way I would have taken on this challenge too.

Yet of all years, God—in his all-knowing sovereignty—knew this year was the one when we needed to focus on transforming our insides, while so much of our outside world was crumbling. Like I reminded my daughter, love, joy, peace, patience, kindness, goodness, faithfulness, gentleness, and self-control in all things—including grumbling—don't come from our efforts. They come from God.

If I had attempted to make it through this year on my own strength, I would have fallen flat on my face. But God knew. He knew he had more of himself to show me. When I had more than I could handle—when I didn't know if I could make it through to the next day—God showed me he was all I needed. In fact, he was more than I needed.

Inside I'm a lot like my daughter. I want the glory without the pain. I want positive attention for my gifts and abilities. I want to be seen and—even though I don't need the paparazzi or the glamour of being famous—I want others to notice me and say, "Well done."

Instead, those who walked through this year with me witnessed something different. They saw someone who did her best but still needed a lot of help. They saw that I couldn't do it all myself. They witnessed me doing the best that I could, while still attempting not to grumble and guiding my children to do the same.

I do think it would have been quite an accomplishment to have worked on not grumbling through any ordinary Goyer year, but God wanted to show our family more. He wanted to show me more. He wanted to show me that even when I'm too exhausted to make it through the day without asking a friend for prayer, or to babysit, or to come and sit with my grandma so I can run to the store, God is still exactly what I needed. And because I had him to lean on, I could be thankful and not grumble because Jesus is more than enough.

It reminds me of one of my favorite stories in the Bible, the story of Jesus raising Lazarus from the dead. If anyone was seeking fame and attention, raising a man from the dead would certainly get it. I'm sure the word got out! Yet that wasn't Jesus' motivation. Why did Jesus do what he did? We don't have to guess on this one because he tells us in his Word. As I pondered my daughter's desire for fame, I turned back to the story.

A man named Lazarus was sick. He lived in Bethany with his sisters, Mary and Martha. This is the Mary who later poured the expensive perfume on the Lord's feet and wiped them with her hair. Her brother, Lazarus, was sick. So the two sisters sent a message to Jesus telling him, "Lord, your dear friend is very sick."

But when Jesus heard about it he said, "Lazarus's sickness will not end in death. No, it happened for the glory of God so that the Son of God will receive glory from this." So although Jesus loved Martha, Mary, and Lazarus, he stayed where he was for the next two days. Finally, he said to his disciples, "Let's go back to Judea." (John 11:1–7 NLT)

Mary and Martha had a great need—their brother was very sick. They sent word to Jesus, and my guess was they had a plan for how things were going to turn out. Jesus would get the message, he'd come immediately, and he'd revive Lazarus with his healing touch, just as they'd seen him do many times.

Maybe, as they waited, the sisters sent a servant to the door to watch for Jesus' coming. Maybe the sisters took turns watching for him themselves. Yet hours passed, then days, and the only thing that met them at the door was disappointment. They had no idea what Jesus had planned; all they knew was that during their waiting time hope ran out, and their brother died.

I can imagine the tears and questions. My guess is that they could see nothing good coming from their brother dying. Yet Jesus saw things differently. This death would lead to a new knowledge of who the sisters thought him to be. This death—like the one it foreshadowed on the cross—would end in a display of God's glory.

Of course God displaying his glory—and his desire for the glory to be his alone—wasn't something new. Man's first corporate sin was trying to steal what rightfully belonged to God alone.

Genesis 11:4 relates, "Then they said, 'Come, let us build ourselves a city, with a tower that reaches to the heavens, so that we may make a name for ourselves; otherwise we will be scattered over the face of the whole earth.'"

Instead of working together to make God's name known, their plan was to work together to make their own names known. It is the same for all the generations to follow. This still continues to be the battle between God and man. We want to take credit for all our greatness, and God wants to get us to the place where his greatness is on display.

Many years after the Tower of Babel, God attempted to get the attention of a prideful people yet again. And he did it by getting them to the place where they couldn't succeed—couldn't live!—without him.

> Then the LORD said to Moses, "Look, I'm going to rain down food from heaven for you. Each day the people can go out and pick up as much food as they need for that day. I will test them in this to see whether or not they will follow my instructions. On the sixth day they will gather food, and when they prepare it, there will be twice as much as usual."
>
> So Moses and Aaron said to all the people of Israel, "By evening you will realize it was the LORD who brought you out of the land of Egypt. In the morning you will see the glory of the LORD, because he has heard your complaints, which are against him, not against us. What have we done that you should complain about us?" (Ex. 16:4–7 NLT)

God showed Mary and Martha his glory by not arriving on their timetable and raising a man from death, instead of healing a man. In the desert God showed the Israelites his glory by providing food from heaven when they had no way to source a supply that could nourish millions. In our home God showed his glory when incident after incident became more than we could handle and we had to look to God for provision, direction, and strength.

When you think about it, when does God's glory show up the best? When we're at the end of ourselves. When we can't provide for our own needs. When we are unsure how we're going to make it through the day. When all our hopes are dead.

And you know what? Even though our family did our best with not grumbling about our circumstances, our complaints, questions, and concerns still came. Starting with mine.

How can I provide care for a bedridden grandmother and still
care for a husband and seven kids at home?
When will I get time to work on book deadlines when I'm
struggling to make sure my kids have dinner on the table
and clean clothes to wear?

My kids had complaints too:

It's not fair that Mom has to stay home and take care of
Grandma, and she can't go to the movies with us, or church,
or take us out for frozen yogurt.
Why can't I join gymnastics or baseball like my friends? Other
moms have time to take their kids to practice.

These complaints may seem shallow, but they are honest and real. And even while we were working not to complain about little stuff, like a sister wearing favorite socks or a brother messing up a LEGO tower, we all still struggled with why the big, hard stuff of life seemed to be slamming us all at once.

We know the Israelites complained too—a lot—but their grumbles were about the ability to sustain life. Being stuck in a desert with a few million of your kissing cousins and no Walmart to stop by for bread and milk was sort of a big deal. The thing is, though, God had already shown up in so many ways (think parting the Red Sea), yet instead of praying and praising they grumbled and complained.

God wasn't going to let his people starve, but they did pay for their grumbling. Because of it, they weren't allowed to enter the promised land. Instead, most of them—except for Joshua and Caleb, who trusted God—died in the desert. If anything, this shows that our words and attitude toward God matter . . . a lot.

Numbers 14:21–24 says:

> Nevertheless, as surely as I live and as surely as the glory of the LORD fills the whole earth, not one of those who saw my glory and the signs I performed in Egypt and in the wilderness but who disobeyed me and tested me ten times—not one of them will ever see the land I promised on oath to their ancestors. No one who has treated me with contempt will ever see it. But because my servant Caleb has a different spirit and follows me wholeheartedly, I will bring him into the land he went to, and his descendants will inherit it.

Yes, God provided daily bread, and, yes, they saw his glory. But still they disobeyed him. Still they tested him with their complaints.

Mary and Martha grumbled too. They believed in who Jesus was, and they knew he was the one they needed. Yet in the middle of their greatest need, he stayed away. And when both women saw Jesus, they made their disappointment in his lack of quick action and consideration known. It is recorded that both of them said the same words: "Lord, if only you had been here, my brother would not have died" (John 11:21, 32 NLT). Yet it was Martha who, even after her complaint, returned to her faith.

> Martha said to Jesus, "Lord, if only you had been here, my brother would not have died. But even now I know that God will give you whatever you ask." (John 11:21–22 NLT)

Martha related that even though she questioned why Jesus didn't come sooner, she trusted he could still be powerful in the situation. Jesus, of course, knew he was powerful. More powerful than she could imagine. And Jesus wanted to show both Martha and Mary that.

> Jesus, once more deeply moved, came to the tomb. It was a cave with a stone laid across the entrance. "Take away the stone," he said.
>
> "But, Lord," said Martha, the sister of the dead man, "by this time there is a bad odor, for he has been there four days."
>
> Then Jesus said, "Did I not tell you that if you believe, you will see the glory of God?"
>
> So they took away the stone. Then Jesus looked up and said, "Father, I thank you that you have heard me. I knew that you always hear me, but I said this for the benefit of the people standing here, that they may believe that you sent me."
>
> When he had said this, Jesus called in a loud voice, "Lazarus, come out!" The dead man came out, his hands and feet wrapped with strips of linen, and a cloth around his face.
>
> Jesus said to them, "Take off the grave clothes and let him go." (John 11:38–44)

Jesus did less than the sisters hoped for when believed they needed him most in order to show them more.

In Matthew Henry's commentary for this passage he wrote, "Let this reconcile us to the darkest dealings of Providence, that they are all for the glory of God: sickness, loss, disappointment, are so; and if God be glorified, we ought to be satisfied. . . . Jesus loved Martha, and her sister, and Lazarus. . . . God has gracious intentions, even when he seems to delay."

Reading that last line resonated with what had been happening throughout the year. Life had brought huge challenges, but God had given me daily bread, providing exactly what I needed for each day, showing me his glory. God had gracious intentions even though I questioned how I would make it through a day.

Through the difficulties, God showed me his glory in heartache. "Did I not tell you that if you believe, you will see the glory of God?" Jesus asked Martha, and I had been there many times over the previous months. Jesus had been asking the same of me—of us.

"You didn't know how you'd get your work done, and I gave you wisdom and strength. You didn't know how you could care for Grandma, and I brought you help. I also brought friends to help pay for her care when you had nothing to pay toward it. I brought you a caregiver, someone you could trust. Someone you could be comfortable with in your home. Did I not tell you that if you believed, you would see the glory of God?"

I thought this year would be more about me not grumbling when I had to stand behind four other people in the Walmart grocery line, but God wanted more for me. He wanted to give me a deeper knowledge of himself, his provision, and his glory. Like Lazarus, I had to die to myself—and die to my ability to help myself—in order to see more of Jesus. I needed to take the spotlight off of me and my talents and point it to my Lord.

I wanted to be able to grumble less and hold my tongue more, but Jesus wanted my earthly nature to die. (Not that it has completely, but it has been knocked down a level or two.)

I wanted to take a challenge, write a book, and be an inspiration for other moms, and God wanted to display his glory and turn the attention back to him—where it needed to be in the first place.

God wanted me to trade in my dreams of fame for his fame. And he wanted me to realize that I needed his help and his strength to do that.

"Putting our earthly nature to death isn't something we can do apart from God," wrote my friend Joanna Weaver in her book *Lazarus Awakening.* "It isn't meant to be a renovation we attempt on our own or a charade we play at until it becomes reality. Believe me, I've tried it that way, and it just doesn't work. And yet, while the Holy Spirit wants to help us, we must initiate the act. For in a very real sense, only we can choose to die."[1]

I was not even within the last few months of this challenge yet, but if I could sum up what I had learned so far, it was that I'd had to choose to die to my own thoughts, ideas, and strengths in order for God to show up.

I wanted a successful year, but Jesus had simply called me to look to him more and more. This reminded me of a quote by Mother Teresa that I always appreciated but now more fully understood: "God has not called me to be successful. He has called me to be faithful."[2]

And we can be faithful, remembering that time after time when we put our trust in Jesus, he will show up. Or, as my pastor/rapper friend Cai Lane says, "The same God that got you through your last challenging season is the same God that blessed you with a season of abundance. Our situation of comfort or discomfort should not impede on our trust in God. God does not switch up."

I thought it was a good teaching moment for my daughter when I sat down to talk to her about fame and our desires, but the more I thought about it, the more I realized that maybe this message was for me too. Maybe for me more.

Reflection Questions

1. When was a time when you waited for God to show up and then learned later that he had something better for you than what you desired?
2. We often want the glory for ourselves, rather than giving glory to God, and we grumble when we don't get what we want. How is giving glory to God the better way?
3. We often want to stop grumbling, but God wants us to die to ourselves. How will our grumbling change as we do?

Your Turn

Take time to memorize Galatians 5:22–23 with your family: "But the fruit of the Spirit is love, joy, peace, forbearance, kindness, goodness, faithfulness, gentleness and self-control. Against such things there is no law." Explain to your kids that the fruit of these actions comes from God. He doesn't require that we work harder to be more loving, joyful, peaceful, forbearing, kind, good, faithful, gentle, or self-controlled. Instead, we need to turn to him and ask him to be these things in us.

Also, talk about biblical people who believed God and those who didn't. What happened to those who dared to believe God? What happened to those who grumbled and complained—what were their rewards and consequences? How can their actions be an example to us of what to do or not to do?

Chapter 16

HAVE WE REALLY CHANGED?

The last few weeks summer had been in full swing, and one of the best parts of summer was having our daughter Leslie in town along with her sister-in-law, Maruška, who was fifteen—the same age as Grace and Maddie. Leslie lives and teaches in the Czech Republic, and this was Maruška's first time in the United States. It was fun seeing our crazy life, our world, through Maruška's eyes. One thing was certain. She was so excited to be with us she never grumbled . . . not once.

With family in town, I wanted a chance for all of us to get away together. So while Kayleigh stayed with Grandma, I booked an Airbnb, and we all traveled to middle-of-nowhere Arkansas for some time together.

The large yellow farmhouse on a hill was filled with noise and overflowed with people. John and I, our seven younger kids, and Leslie and Maruška were all there. Nathan came, too, and Cory came with his two kids, ages four and seven. All the kids loved feeding the horses and goats, catching crawfish in the muddy creek, and chasing fireflies at dusk. I enjoyed the fact that the Wi-Fi was horrible, and in the evenings we played board games since personal devices and television didn't work well. (The older ones did grumble about the lack of Wi-Fi a bit.)

I decided this trip would be the perfect time for us to do a self-evaluation. Over the past few months, I'd noted changes in our family. Had my children seen the same things? Was it all part of my imagination?

I wrote up a questionnaire where the kids rated their grumble score last year and compared it with their score this year. Most of them looked similar to this:

Grace
Grumble score: 5 ⇒ 3

Things I changed: Not complaining about my chores a lot

Things I still need to change: To stop grumbling about my siblings and health issues

Things that help me change: Reading my Bible and praying

Maddie
Grumble score: 7 ⇒ 4

Things I changed: I'm not complaining as much or making rude noises.

Things I still need to change: I need to stop being unthankful. I also need to stop grumbling in my mind.

Things that help me change: Praying to Jesus, asking him to help me stop being unthankful and to stop grumbling

I was happy to see that my kids saw improvement. I also felt they rated themselves fairly well. They didn't see themselves as having arrived. They also saw the solution for grumbling as seeking more help from God through prayer and Bible reading. Little did I know at the time that just a few weeks later, how they handled things—grumbling or not—would be tested.

-☼-

A few weeks after our trip to the farm, we were still looking for fun things to do, especially since Maruška only had a few days left with us before she headed back to the Czech Republic. In my mind an American mall experience was needed. I just had no idea what this would mean for all of us.

I'd heard about the big Build-A-Bear event a few days before it happened. "Pay Your Age Day" meant just that. It sounded fun and affordable. (Build-A-Bears are usually very expensive!) The fun part of Build-A-Bear is you get to pick out your bear, add a cloth heart, and then watch it get stuffed.

I arrived with nine kids, ages four to sixteen years old, thirty minutes before the store opened. I expected we'd have to wait an hour or two. WRONG. By the time we got there, hundreds of families were already in line. The store opened at 10:00 a.m., and we heard people had been lining up since 6:30 that morning. We learned the early bird does get the worm . . . or in this case the bear.

We spent our time in line eating mall food and streaming cartoons on my phone—until my phone died. At first the line seemed to be moving quickly. But we soon figured out that this mostly came from people leaving the line. The closer we got to the front (within a few stores of Build-A-Bear), the slower the line went. Two hours passed, four hours, six . . .

But still we were *so close*. The kids could see into the store. It was easy to focus on the prize and be optimistic when we could see the end goal—to a fault. A few times I asked the kids if they wanted to leave the line. After seven hours, purchasing each one of them a stuffed animal from Walmart seemed like a good idea. But the kids didn't want to give up.

My legs grew tired from standing, and soon we found ourselves sitting on the dirty mall floor. Even though there were thousands of parents and kids there, people treated each other with respect. I saw people doing food runs for others in the line. People also held places when moms needed to take kids on bathroom breaks. People chatted and joked with each other. Overall, people, even strangers, do care for each other. My friends cared for me well too. One friend brought snacks and crafts for my kids. Another brought me a coffee. And another came to visit me in line.

What impressed me the most, though, was that the kids were resilient. They played with other kids. They made up a game with a coin that they played for an hour. For the most part they didn't whine and complain.

And then the time neared when we were right at the door. Nine hours had passed, and we were the next family in line. We'd made it! They were only letting in fifteen people at a time, and as I stood there it was clear why the line had taken so long. It took three to four minutes to stuff each bear with the machine. This was no fast task.

It was eight at night, and a long, long line still stretched behind us. Hundreds of people still waited. I wondered how the store's staff would handle this. Surely they wouldn't send everyone away.

Three security guards stood at the door, and for the last hour we'd witnessed them being harassed by some of the people behind us. Even though our group had been patient and hadn't grumbled, some people behind us weren't acting as nice. And these were grown adults. I noticed the shock on my kids' faces to see adults acting that way.

The security guards looked as weary as I felt. And as we stood there—with our toes on the threshold of the store—the guards' radios started squawking. I couldn't hear what they were saying, but the guards looked at the line, then moved to talk to the store staff. Concern matched the weariness on their faces, and my heart sank.

Please don't close the door and send us away. Please don't say they won't let any more people in.

As I tried to listen to the conversation and watch their faces, my kids were focused on the prize ahead. They chatted about what bears they wanted to choose. All their weariness had washed away when they saw all those teddy bears within arm's reach.

The staff and the guards seemed to come to some type of decision, and one of the guards approached.

My hand gripped the shoulders of Aly, who stood in front of me. My heart pounded with worry over what he was about to say.

"What's happening?" I asked.

"Well, ma'am, we're going to let you all in in a few minutes, but we had to make a decision. They'll let you purchase a bear, but you won't be able to get them stuffed tonight."

"What?" Alexis' voice cried out. "That's not fair!"

I shushed her.

"We have all these people behind y'all that need bears. We want to make sure they get them tonight." He rubbed his weary brow. "But the folks here said you can come back another day to get them filled."

Nine sets of eyes looked to me in confusion.

"What is he saying?"

"What does that mean?"

"Are we not getting stuffed bears tonight?"

The youngest kids broke into tears, and my heart broke for them.

"Look at me. Listen to me." My voice was soft. "I know you've been here all day. And we are the next ones in line. All of us will be able to go in and pick out a bear . . . but we won't be able to get it stuffed now."

"Why can't they just let us go next and get ours stuffed?" Aly asked. "We're right here."

"Honey, they had to stop somewhere. And we just happened to be the ones they stopped at."

Sissy pouted and glared into the store at the people who'd been just in front of us all day. They waited and watched as their bears were getting stuffed with fluff, excitement on their faces. "But that's not fair!" she cried.

"I know, but if we got them stuffed, it wouldn't be fair to the people in line behind us."

I sighed, and my mind scurried for a way to help my kids. Inwardly, I laughed to myself. *Of course we're doing the Grumble-Free Year and this happens . . . to be the next ones in line. Unbelievable.*

I composed myself.

"Listen, I know you're all disappointed, but remember what we've been working on? Not grumbling. Remember what we learned? True character is shown when we're tired or disappointed. In this case we're both. But this is our opportunity. We can grumble, or we can be thankful. We made it this far. We will get bears. In fact, we can say this is the best day ever."

"Best day ever." Sissy sighed. "Yeah, right."

I forced a smile. "Well, it could be. We got to spend the whole day together. We got to eat lots of mall food. You've made new friends. You'll get a bear . . . a flat bear. And remember, I told you we'll get McFlurries when we're done. What could be better than that? Best day ever!"

The tears stopped as I pointed inside toward the bins of flat bears. "We'll come back to get them fluffed up. Which one are you going to get?"

The tears from a moment before dried up, replaced once again by excited chatter.

The security guards moved down the line, telling others what we'd just learned. Everyone would get bears, but they'd have to come back to get them stuffed. Thankfully my kids were so excited about finally getting into the store that they didn't notice the angry shouts from those in line behind us.

As we entered the store, the older kids started a chant. The younger ones joined in. "Best day ever. Best day ever." We picked out our bears and purchased them. We ate McFlurries, then we posed for photos with flat bears when we got home.

There were a few more tears that night from the youngest kids. After all, flat bears are hard to cuddle with, and they were exhausted. But overall I was impressed. All we'd been working on over the last ten months had made a difference.

I was reminded of how much my attitude changed everything. When I joked about only making it ten feet forward in line in one hour's time, my kids did too.

When we got to the front of the line, and they told us they would no longer be stuffing bears, my kids were rightfully upset. Yet when I smiled and told my kids that true character is shown when we're exhausted and disappointed, they really took that to heart. I told them it was easy to be thankful when circumstances were uncomplicated, but we can still be thankful even when it's hard. And my kids followed my example. So much, in fact, that on the way home we continued to cheer, "Best day ever!"

We never started off planning to spend all day in line at Build-A-Bear. If someone had told me we'd spend ten and a half hours and end up with unstuffed bears, I would have said, "No way."

Looking back, I'm not sure I'd do it again, but I truly believe it was a day my kids will never forget. These types of memories are priceless, especially when we experience them without grumbles.

⋆

The thing about unexpected challenges is that they're unexpected. If I'd known it would have taken ten hours to get an unstuffed bear, we never would have gone. Yet if we hadn't gone, my kids never would have had the chance to do a 180-degree turn on their attitudes. Out of all the thousands of people in line that day, the stuffing stopped at us. What were the odds of that?

The Bible, of course, doesn't talk about chance. Instead, it talks about providence. Things don't happen because of a cosmic roll of the dice. Instead, we can trust there is a God who looks over us, who cares.

That night we all went to bed knowing that no matter what happened, we were cared for by a loving God. I mean, face it, many people in this world have far bigger struggles than unstuffed bears, and God knows and cares for them too.

Luke 12:6–7 says, "Are not five sparrows sold for two pennies? And not one of them is forgotten before God. Why, even the hairs of your head are all numbered. Fear not; you are of more value than many sparrows" (ESV).

My goal during the summer was to create memorable experiences for my kids, and I guarantee as long as we live no one will forget that day and the flat bears that lay limply on our laps on the way home.

So even though my kids rated their grumble scores as higher than they would have liked after all that time, I still counted our journey as a win. The value of such a challenge may not be in always getting it right but in pulling it together during hard times when it really matters.

Reflection Questions

1. Sometimes it's hard to see how we've changed or improved. In what ways do you evaluate changes in your life?
2. How does a parent's attitude toward a hard situation change everything?
3. In what ways does constant training help our kids—and us—over time?

Your Turn

The hardest challenges to overcome are ones we don't expect, yet even then we can focus on turning hard days into good ones . . . and maybe even turning them into the "best day ever."

Get some 3 x 5 cards and write "Best Day Ever" on them. Tuck one in your purse. Put another up on your fridge. Use those as a reminder that you can turn things around.

When we're tired and overwhelmed, it's easy to allow our grumbles to take control. Instead, try to turn a bad situation around for the good. And if you succeed, give yourself a pat on the back for that.

Chapter 17

SOMETIMES THE GRUMBLES GO DEEPER THAN WE THINK

There were a few weeks when one of my teens had been acting uncharacteristically distant. When I tried to talk to her about normal things like her laundry, chores, or what we were having for dinner, she had an attitude. A bad, bad attitude. Outbursts were followed by mouthiness and anger toward siblings and parents alike. But the bulk of it came my way.

Usually when my kids got mouthy or angry, I was the target. Their dad rarely came under fire unless he defended me, which had become the case more than once in the last few days. It took all of my self-control to put aside my own feelings and instead try to understand what was going on with my kid.

Finally, after days of me asking what was wrong, my daughter sat down to tell us how she felt. As she did, tears poured out with her words.

She shared with us the guilt she felt over her adoption and her longing for her biological parents. Even though my mind told me it was good for her to open up about all the things stuffed deep inside, my heart didn't like to hear the words. I wished my love made all the difference. I wished that finalized adoption papers meant that the pain of the past was wiped away, old wounds were instantly healed, and new bonds were connected with super glue. None of those things was the case.

It was a good reminder to look beyond the grumbles. My daughter's attitude wasn't just about her complaining. It was an invitation for me to step closer, to dig deeper, and to attempt to figure out what was really going on. To care about her hurt and to not take her actions or emotions personally.

From the beginning I'd had to learn this. Our adopted daughters often hid the truth because they didn't know how to share what was really on their hearts. And grumbling, in a way, was easier than sharing all the hurt deep inside.

⁻ᵇ⁻

We'd only interacted with our soon-to-be adopted daughters a few times before we were allowed to bring them home for a weekend visit. On the drive to our house, twelve-year-old Maddie bounced in her seat with excitement.

"I'm going to be such a big helper. I'll help you with anything you ask. You saved my life . . . I'm going to always be thankful," she said with a squeal.

Sure enough, when we arrived home, she didn't leave my side as I made dinner.

"Do you need help with anything else?" she'd ask after completing each task.

"Sure, can you wash that bowl real quick so I can make a salad?"

"Yes, ma'am," she said with enthusiasm. "I'll do anything you ask. I will always be thankful you're adopting us."

I knew with these girls there would be a honeymoon period. I guessed they would be on their best behavior for a few weeks, and then—when they got comfortable—things would change. Looking back I wish that honeymoon period would have lasted a few weeks. Instead, it was a few hours, and then the fighting, grumbling, and complaining began. Not only did the girls not act thankful, there were times I doubted they wanted to be with us at all. Big blowups would happen over little things. And they grumbled about bedtime and chores.

The little kids also grumbled. Mostly because they had to share the TV and our time. It seemed like much of our days were spent trying to bring peace. The adjustment was bigger than I expected, and I grew completely exhausted.

I wish I could say that I found a quick fix, but mostly I began to understand (after months and months of therapy) what the grumbles were about. First, there was fear. These kids had been hurt so many times that they expected things to go wrong. They expected us to get tired of them. They waited for the time when one of their angry episodes would be the last straw and we'd tell them we'd changed our minds about the adoption.

The honeymoon stage turned into a time of them testing us over and over again—acting out to see if we truly meant what we said about being a forever family. They'd act out in big ways and grumble in small ones, and I often found myself grumbling too.

Second, the mumbles and the grumbles came from a lack of trust. One daughter in particular struggled with this. For most of her life she'd felt as though she was a burden to people. She was the one who was often sent to a different foster home for her behavior. She was the one who was separated from her sisters for much of the time. And instead of making her needs known and asking for something, she'd just grumble about not having it.

If six other kids asked for ice cream and got it, instead of asking for it, too, she'd grumble that she didn't have any. She found it hard to trust people. It was hard for her to tell who really had her best intentions in mind and who didn't.

Finally, the grumbles came from a sense of loss. This realization probably took me the longest to understand. As an adoptive mom I wanted to believe that all my love would wash away all their pain. Yes, they'd had a hard life, but look at all they had now! I wanted them to act like Maddie did on that first day: simply thankful for what we offered them.

It took a while for me to see that many times the grumbles we express have little to do with what's currently happening. They can come from past hurts, old memories, or unfulfilled expectations. Trust takes time to build, and we were still in the process of building it.

Over time we legally became a forever family, and healing began layer by layer. With this healing came more contentment. And when things felt better inside, soon outward reactions began to change.

One especially hard day with Maddie made me feel as if we hadn't been working on being grumble-free for months and months already. She acted mad the moment she woke up. She grumbled about what I'd made for breakfast and complained when I told the kids it was time to sit down and start homeschool.

She verbally poked at her siblings, stirring their anger, and ended up getting them mad too. It was only after I got frustrated, yelled, and took away her privileges for electronics that I began to wonder what was really going on. A few more arguments and a few hours later, she finally confessed to me that she'd had a dream about her past that really bothered her. Looking back I wish I'd pulled her aside right from the beginning and urged her to tell me what was going on.

I'm trying to do better. I'm trying to see my daughters' attitudes as a signal that I need to reach out to them, not just react to them. There is usually a deeper reason for what's going on.

Thankfully . . .

God can help.
God can help my child control her tongue.
God can help me control my tongue.
God can help me know when to offer a little more compassion.
God gives compassion to me as I deal with my kids.
God can heal us all. Layer by layer.

※

Maybe you're looking at the grumbling in your house and wondering if you'll ever have the right answer to stop all the drama and all the fuss. Or maybe—like me—you'll realize the grumbling is simply an outward sign of the layers of pain inside. Maybe one of your family members sees grumbling as an acceptable way to deal with all the anxiety, pain, and uncertainty they don't know how to deal with.

Yet, whether we're dealing with a bad habit or with a deeper issue, there is one place we can turn: God. It's in him we can put our trust.

I didn't always have the answers for our grumbles. I also didn't always have the answers for my daughter's anxiety and pain. Often the best answer was just to let my daughter know that God was there and he cared.

John was good at this. He had a gentle way of putting an arm around one of our kids and talking to them in soft tones. Often, while I was trying to figure out solutions, he was simply offering time and attention. His gentleness let those he cared about know that they didn't have to be perfect to be receivers of his love—or of God's.

I have offered ideas and solutions in so many places in this book, but sometimes the best thing to do is none of it. Sometimes the best way to help our kids is not to try to help them or solve their problems but simply to be available. As a person who likes to fix things, this is hard. Yet it's easier to calm our grumbles when we know we are adored. I'm trying to remember to do that more, or rather to do less, so that I can show my kids that they are loved just for who they are.

Reflection Questions

1. When was a time that you focused on the grumbles only to discover something deeper was going on?

2. What is a strategy for reaching out to a grumbling person with gentleness instead of reacting to them?
3. What things could be impacting your family or friends at this time, causing them to grumble?

Your Turn

Next time you're dealing with a grumbling person, don't try to fix it. Instead, just be loving and available. Offer open arms. Remember that often our kids grumble because it's easier to do than to share what's really going on. Next time your child has a "grumbling problem," pause and ask a few questions:

- What is really going on?
- How can I draw close and let my child know I care?
- How can I show my child love, even in the midst of this grumbling attitude?

Drawing close is often the hardest thing to do, but often it's the only thing that allows you to get to the heart of the problem.

Chapter 18

THE DAY THAT COULD HAVE CHANGED EVERYTHING

When I first considered writing *The Grumble-Free Year*, I learned a new term: *social experiment book*. Basically it's a research project or experiment conducted with human subjects (in this case, my family) in the real world. In our experiment, we lived our normal lives while also attempting to learn to live grumble-free. In most cases I was doing the guiding, teaching, and discipling, but sometimes my kids brought in their observations from the real world.

The thing about social experiment books is that you never know what's going to happen in a year. Like Proverbs 16:9 says, "We can make our plans, but the LORD determines our steps" (NLT). This year, whenever I thought we'd moved past the hard stuff and were settling into a routine, something else would happen.

Big stuff. Hard stuff. Unexpected stuff. Through it all, I came to realize one thing: it's not only important not to grumble; it's also important to be thankful for everything. It's the hard stuff that makes us lean into Christ like never before. It also makes us draw closer to our family, realizing the importance of walking through life together. Still, it never makes the hard stuff any easier to go through. Like today.

Today was a day I'd been looking forward to for a while. Since I homeschool my kids, I'm with them 24–7, but back in April I had carved out some time for me—hopefully time to get some writing done. Looking ahead, I had scheduled *four whole days* when all of my kids would be in summer day camp. And for two of those days, Grandma would be at therapy, which meant I'd have the house all to myself. It would be like a dream.

The first day I knew I wouldn't get much alone time because I'd just be getting back from my writers retreat. But July 24 would be my day . . . until I realized my husband had scheduled his colonoscopy that day and needed me to drive him. But there was even a problem with that. Since I had Grandma to get ready and out the door for her therapy bus and six kids to get to their day camps, I couldn't give John a ride to his appointment. Instead, Nathan took John to the hospital. The plan was that I'd pick up John after his procedure, we'd go out to eat, and then we'd head home. John would go back to work, and I'd have the whole quiet house to myself after that. It still seemed like a workable plan.

On the way to the hospital to pick up John, I listened to one of my favorite podcasts, *The Happy Hour with Jamie Ivey*. The guest was Brittany Price Brooker, a mom who was widowed with three kids when she was only twenty-five years old.[1] As I listened, my heart ached for that young woman.

I can't imagine, I thought as I pictured my tribe at home. John is my rock, the playful one, and the peacemaker who keeps our family steady when the kids get out of hand and I get overwhelmed. I listened—with tears in my eyes—as I neared the hospital. I had no idea that at that very moment my own husband was having a crisis during a routine procedure. When I got to the waiting room, a doctor was there to tell me that John had stopped breathing and had to be resuscitated.

Resuscitated? John stopped breathing on the table? My heartbeat quickened with fear, and my knees trembled as I sank down into the waiting room chair.

The doctor told me I could go back to see him soon, and as I waited I watched, numb, as a half-dozen people circled around the recovery area. I thought about Brittany's story from moments before, realizing anew how fragile life is. Brittany's story could have been my story. This morning when I kissed John goodbye could have been our last.

Thank you, God, for keeping him here. I need him. I can't do this life without my husband.

I placed a hand over a growing knot in my stomach. How much time, focus, and emotions had I wasted on things that didn't really matter? Just that morning I'd grumbled to myself about having to waste "my" free day going to the hospital to give John a ride home. I'd felt cheated about that hour I'd had to give up, and then, as I rushed into the recovery area where John lay in the hospital, I simply wanted to grab my husband's hand, to feel its warmth. My husband's eyes were puffy, and his face was flushed from the medications they'd shot into his lungs to revive him, but seeing his slight smile made my heart flip.

The doctor entered a moment later and told us John would have to stay in the hospital awhile to recover, and thankfulness flooded my heart. I realized how much was perfectly in place for this exact situation. During the coming days when I needed to be at John's side, all my childcare was already covered by day camps. I'd scheduled that time to give myself a break, but God had known all those months prior what I'd really need the time for. *Thank you, Lord.*

After the initial scare, I faced the reality of John staying in the hospital. He'd thrown up while in surgery and had aspirated the vomit into his lungs, and it was turning into an infection. But at least I hadn't lost him. At least I could be thankful things hadn't turned out worse.

All these things were on my mind when I kissed my husband goodbye and left him at the hospital to return home to the kids. Amazingly, everyone was in a good mood. Even though all the kids were concerned about their dad, they didn't argue or complain. When I asked them to go to bed, I was met by "Yes, ma'am," and no one grumbled. It's as if everyone realized it had been a hard day and we really didn't need to grumble about the little stuff. We were all just thankful that Dad was okay.

We grumble about so many little things in life and often don't think twice about it. It becomes our go-to attitude. Even though I'd been working at it this year, I was still not perfect. I still grumbled, usually about the messes in the house. But overall, I wanted to be a light. As Philippians 2:13–16 says:

> For it is God who works in you, both to will and to work for his good pleasure.
>
> Do all things without grumbling or disputing, that you

may be blameless and innocent, children of God without blemish in the midst of a crooked and twisted generation, among whom you shine as lights in the world, holding fast to the word of life, so that in the day of Christ I may be proud that I did not run in vain or labor in vain. (ESV)

When we are grumble-free, we are a light to the world. We look different and sound different, and it is noticeable. Particularly in this imperfect world we live in where hard things happen out of nowhere. I want to be known as a positive person who encouraged and supported others.

The first night of John's hospital stay, I was home with all my kids. My youngest daughter said she had a stomachache and wanted to sleep with me. I had a feeling it had more to do with her dad being in the hospital than anything else. In addition, the puppy—who usually slept in his crate—darted under the bed and wouldn't come out. I had no doubt the puppy knew something was going on too.

Then, in the middle of the night, the puppy started whining and needed to be let out. As I grabbed my phone to check the time, I saw a Voxer notification from a prayer group I'm a part of. Wondering about the prayer need in the middle of the night, I was heartbroken to read that my friend Wynter Pitts had suddenly and unexpectedly passed away, presumably from a heart attack. My heart sank. I dropped to my knees in shock.

How could that be? Wynter was young. She was an author, speaker, magazine founder—doing so much to serve families, especially young girls. She was a wife and mother of four daughters. How could she be gone?

The next day, as her death was announced to the public, her uncle Tony Evans had this to say of her: "Wynter was bright, loyal, generous, diligent, and simply a delight. A treasured part of our family." And that's how I remembered her too. Kind, thoughtful, and caring—someone who loved Jesus. And someone who was with Jesus now.

I considered my own legacy. *How do I want to be remembered? How will my light shine?*

After I dropped off all my kids at their camps, I drove to see John. As I drove, worship songs filled my mind and flowed out from my lips. And amazingly, even through this new trial, I trusted God even more than I had before.

A verse came to mind. First Corinthians 1:7–9 says:

> Therefore you do not lack any spiritual gift as you eagerly wait
> for our Lord Jesus Christ to be revealed. He will also keep you
> firm to the end, so that you will be blameless on the day of
> our Lord Jesus Christ. God is faithful, who has called you into
> fellowship with his Son, Jesus Christ our Lord.

God was available to complete the work in me, no matter what trials and sufferings came in the midst of a year, a month, a day. I could stand firm, not because of what was or wasn't going on around me. Instead, I could stand firm because of who Jesus is.

As my friend Mary DeMuth said in her podcast *Pray Every Day*, which I had been listening to as I drove to the hospital:

> It's soul-settling to know we don't have to be our own rock.
> Instead, Jesus promises he is that rock. In this life, storms will
> rage all around us, but when they do, we can look down at our
> feet and see that it's Jesus the rock we're standing upon—the
> safest place on earth.

This year had been filled with many storms. Some days it seemed more had gone wrong than right, and I'd certainly wanted to grumble as we faced this new challenge concerning my husband's health. Yet peace came, assurance came, faith came when I took time to look down at my feet and saw solid ground. Saw that it was Jesus I was standing on.

And even though the year had been hard, I realized how all the things I'd wanted to grumble about the day before John's procedure were minor, meaningless things.

The day I had arrived home from my four-day writers retreat I had attempted to have a joyful heart. I knew John had done his best to make sure the house was picked up when I was gone (which meant the living room and kitchen were somewhat clean), and he'd even done four loads of laundry (and the clothes were folded on the chairs in the living room). Yet four days away still meant there were messes in every part of the house.

When I walked into the upstairs bathroom, which is shared by six kids, it was obvious the kids hadn't been doing their chores. My teens are supposed to rotate cleaning the bathroom each day, but from the look of the pile of towels and clothes on the floor—and the mess on the counters and in the tub—it was clear that hadn't been done.

I reminded myself over and over again not to grumble. I reminded myself that for every day I was gone, it took that many days to get back to normal again, so in this case it would take four days.

Since I'd taken a red-eye flight and had gotten very little sleep, I told myself I'd have time the next day to clean after I picked John up from his procedure. Instead, I ended up staying with John at the hospital that day, and the next, and the next. By this point it didn't matter that the house was a huge mess. I was simply thankful my husband was all right.

That night I posted on Facebook: "Yesterday I was overwhelmed by the laundry and messy house after being gone for four days. Today I'm thankful my husband is alive. #perspective #thankyouJesus"

⁃⚙⁃

The same day my husband's breathing stopped, my friend took her last breath. The reality that I could have been mourning my spouse that day hit me hard. Yet even when fears and worries tried to invade (how would I care for all these kids alone?), I turned my focus to the only one sure thing in my life: no matter what happened to my family, friends, or myself, God is—and will ever be—faithful.

- No matter what, his "goodness and love will follow me all the days of my life" (Ps. 23:6).
- No matter what, God said, "I will strengthen you and help you; I will uphold you with my righteous right hand" (Isa. 41:10).
- No matter what, I know God will meet all my needs, "according to the riches of his glory in Christ Jesus" (Phil. 4:19).
- No matter what, the Lord my God is in my midst, a mighty one who will save, rejoicing over me with gladness and quieting me with his love (Zeph. 3:17).

And that's what I felt that day. I was quieted by God's love. I could have grumbled that I lost my "me week," but that seemed foolish since I could have lost my husband. In the upcoming days I could have grumbled about hospital food, uncomfortable hospital chairs, or the time it took driving back and forth to the hospital, but those things didn't matter. My heart was filled with gratitude that we had a hospital to go to and dedicated staff to care for my husband. Even my husband did not grumble—not about being hospitalized, or missing work, or feeling horrible. Whenever I asked how he was doing, he'd offer a pitiful smile. "I'm fine, fine."

More than that, John used his hospital bed as a platform to share the goodness of God. Since it was always quite the production whenever I, or my son Nathan, brought the kids to visit, people began asking questions like, "Are all of these your kids?" or "What made you decide to adopt?" And even though John was winded from the pneumonia in his lungs, he'd spend the next ten, fifteen, twenty minutes sharing about all God had done in our lives and in our family.

I heard from both those who stopped by to visit John and family who called to check on him that even though they'd intended to see how he was doing, they were the ones encouraged or blessed. This is what happens when we choose to praise and be thankful instead of grumble. We become lights in a dark world, even from a hospital bed.

Over the last year I'd come to realize that when I grumbled and complained it indicated I wasn't content with what God was doing in my life. Yes, the grumbles may have seemed to crop up around messes, but deep down my heart was saying, *I shouldn't have to deal with this, God. Things should be easier. Why can't you make things easier?*

John Piper says, "Grumbling is an evidence of little faith in the gracious providence of God in all the affairs of our lives. And little faith is a dishonor to him. It belittles his sovereignty and wisdom and goodness."[2]

If our faith is strong, we will not grumble. As we cease to grumble, our faith becomes stronger.

Even in that hospital bed, John's positive attitude and thankfulness to God pointed to God's gracious providence. And as I looked on the faces of the nurses, doctors, and attendants enraptured by my husband's stories of God's faithfulness to our family, I couldn't help but think, *The person hearing this message of hope may be the one reason our family is going through this trial right now.* And if one person's heart was softened toward God, wouldn't that be worth my sacrificing the "quiet time" I had planned? Of course.

It was amazing to see my husband's faith strong, even though his body was weak, and I knew where that strength was coming from.

We don't always have to be strong in our own strength. We simply need to always remember where to seek our strength from—whom to seek our strength from. John's physical weakness allowed God to be strong in him. As 1 Corinthians 1:25 says, "This foolish plan of God is wiser than the wisest of human plans, and God's weakness is stronger than the greatest of human strength" (NLT).

So whether or not we ended up coming out of this year with less grumbling and more thankfulness, it would all come down to one thing: dependence on Jesus. "Therefore, as it is written: 'Let the one who boasts boast in the Lord'" (1 Cor. 1:31).

As we read through the pages of the Bible, we see that God didn't choose the strong men, the eloquent men, or the perfect men to share his good news and to shed a light in the darkness. Instead, he chose those who were weak, who fumbled with their words, and who messed up a lot. And, in our case, he chose a too-big family, living in a too-small house, with a lot of past trauma—and who still faced daily challenges—as the ones to share God's goodness through the simple task of not grumbling but being thankful instead.

Reflection Questions

1. How does losing someone unexpectedly make us more aware of how often we grumble about meaningless things?
2. When you look down at your feet during trials, what do you find yourself standing on?
3. How does God show himself to be strong in your weaknesses?

Your Turn

You don't have to wait to face huge trials to turn to God. Daily we find ourselves weak. Daily we discover our need for God's strength.

In a journal or a notebook, write out 1 Corinthians 1:25: "This foolish plan of God is wiser than the wisest of human plans, and God's weakness is stronger than the greatest of human strength" (NLT). Then write out a list of things you need wisdom about and another list of areas in which you need strength. Pray that God can help you with both. Consider helping your older kids make lists of their own, focusing on these things.

Then, whenever you find yourself starting to grumble about any of these things, return to this scripture. Turn your thoughts back to God and his perfect plans. Ask him to help you be strong, even in your weaknesses.

Part III

WINDING DOWN

Chapter 19

SELF-DISCIPLINE AND HEART CHANGES

The Grumble-Free Year was coming to a close, and amazingly we'd had the best week out of all of them recently. Our huge family may not have become completely grumble-free, but overall there had been a noticeable difference. A few examples: All my kids did their chores (when reminded) without grumbling. Maddie wanted to go to a sleepover, and when I told her I needed an hour to think about it, she accepted that answer without complaining. When Grace realized Maddie wasn't around to do her part of the kitchen cleanup (because she was at the sleepover), Grace did her chore *and* Maddie's chore without being asked: "Just to help you out, Mom."

Of course there was still some grumbling. One of the little girls whined about wanting an extra snack, and Alexis complained about having to do her own laundry. Whenever I heard these grumbles,

I pointed them out, knowing that every moment was a teaching moment. And there will probably be teaching moments for years to come.

I know this because when I pointed out Alexis's grumbles to her, she said, "But, Mom, I wasn't grumbling to you. I was just grumbling to myself." I took note of that, knowing it was yet another thing to talk about. After all, grumbling is grumbling whether you're doing it to a whole room of people or just in the laundry room when you're by yourself . . . or even if it's just in your head.

One reason it had been a good week overall, though, was that my older girls had been at tae kwon do camp, and their teacher worked hard to nip grumbling in the bud. In fact, Miss Cindy had her students repeat the same mantra every class at the beginning and at the end.

Never give up.
Whatever you start you must finish.
Have a good heart and have a good mind.

This is something that perhaps I need to repeat morning and night, because it's exactly what we've learned on our journey.

Never give up.

Choosing a goal is the easy part; following through day by day is the challenge. Second Timothy 4:7 says, "I have fought the good fight, I have finished the race, and I have remained faithful" (NLT).

Faithfulness is hard to find in this world—whether it is to

marriage, friendship, or a commitment to God. Faithfulness is staying in there for the fight. Faithfulness is finishing the race.

This year there had been many obstacles slowing me down, but I was thankful that, even though there were times I was weary and burdened, I didn't give up. Sure, everyone would have understood if I had—I mean, one person can only tackle so much in a year—but I would have known I'd given up. My children would have known. Who knows? Maybe someday in life—even when I'm not around—when my kids think about giving up, they'll remember that crazy year when they decided not to grumble and persevered despite large, unexpected, and overwhelming challenges.

Whatever you start you must finish.

While this seems to essentially say the same thing as "never give up," my mind focuses on the *start* in this saying. Our family started this grumble-free challenge only because God started it first. From before our births God had an image in mind of who we could be, and the only way we can discover it is to come to a place where we acknowledge the good future God has designed for us, agree with it, and join in the journey of working toward becoming God's best.

Becoming a thankful person, not a grumbling person, was God's idea first. And when I worked to finish what I'd started, I was doing so in agreement with God, who desired this outcome for me before I was even aware of it. As Philippians 1:6 says, "And I am certain that God, who began the good work within you, will continue his work until it is finally finished on the day when Christ Jesus returns" (NLT).

I won't start anything unless it is worth finishing, and God won't either. Remembering this, we can see ourselves always as works in progress. We don't have to worry about trying to be perfect now, yet we can trust that what God started will be finished on the day we finally get to see Jesus face-to-face. And because we have lived our lives turning to him, depending on him, and being faithful to become more like him, what we are given now will open the doors to what God will do in us and through us in the future.

As Matthew 25:23 says, "The master said, 'Well done, my good and faithful servant. You have been faithful in handling this small amount, so now I will give you many more responsibilities. Let's celebrate together!'" (NLT)

I have no doubt that the faithfulness and dedication we all are discovering now will be building blocks for what God wants to do in the future.

Have a good heart and have a good mind.

As we saw on this journey, everything we accomplished had only been done as we centered our hearts and minds in the right place. Salvation only comes when our heart and mind are both engaged, and this is true as we strive to be more Christlike. While our hearts echo our need, desire, and hope for change, our minds remind us that hope is found in Jesus.

And, as I've repeatedly told my children, what's on the inside will come out. What we think and believe will be reflected in our actions. True outward changes only come when we seek God, ask him for more of his Spirit, and then let the fruit of Jesus-in-us flow from our lives.

Yet this doesn't mean we keep on living any way we like until we sense a change inside. It's a double-sided process. We set goals and outwardly work toward achieving them while also seeking God on the inside.

We never would have gotten anywhere this year if we'd kept our mouths grumbling while we waited for inner strength to magically bloom and the desire not to grumble anymore to grow on its own. The outward led to a need for help with the inward, and as we sought the inward, we became better at the outward.

I was reminded of this recently at one of our tae kwon do practices. When two of my teens were grumbling and complaining in the midst of a training class, they turned to their teacher for help, wanting her to pick sides and deal with the other person. With all seriousness Miss Cindy looked at them and said, "I have two words for you: shut up."

I love that. So many of our problems can be solved if we just stop moving our lips. The amazing thing was that my daughters actually listened to her, shut their mouths, and stopped fighting. To witness it was a miracle, really. Compared with three years ago, minor fights like that would have turned into big altercations and escalated quickly. It would have taken fifteen to thirty minutes to break up an argument and then hours (if not days) to get everyone's emotions settled and people talking decently again.

Sometimes, when we find ourselves caught up in the bad habit we're working so hard to kill, we just need to stop doing it. Seal the lips. Stop the negative thoughts. Keep ourselves from acting out until our hearts and minds catch up.

And it wasn't just their tae kwon do teacher that my kids were listening to more consistently now but me as well. More than once in the last week one child said something rude to another, and I commented, "That didn't sound very nice," or "That didn't seem like the best way you could say that."

And then the child responded, "You're right. That didn't sound nice. I'm sorry."

I had to stop myself from displaying a shocked expression on my face when I heard these types of responses. Instead, I simply sent up a prayer of thankfulness that God was working in my kids' hearts and minds. It gave me the extra oomph I needed as a mom to continue being diligent in training them, to not give up, and to finish what I started—with them and with myself—with God's help.

-☼-

I have to admit, when our family started the Grumble-Free Year, I was after one thing: less grumbling. I liked the idea of not having to deal with discontented and dissatisfied kids. I was weary of the bellyaching, bemoaning, and bickering. It was only through the process that I discovered how grumbling makes our hearts weak and how gratitude makes us strong instead.

I also learned how much God is there to help. As 2 Chronicles 16:9 says, "The eyes of the LORD search the whole earth in order to strengthen those whose hearts are fully committed to him" (NLT).

God is searching. God is alert to those who are in need of strength and those who know that strength only comes from God himself.

I came up with lots of Bible readings, lessons, and ideas to help me train and disciple my children, and all of that was good. But where God really worked is when I came to the end of myself and was greatly in need of strength, and—instead of grumbling—I turned to him.

I wanted an easier life, but God gave me what I really needed: full commitment and full satisfaction in him. Not only did I grumble less, but, following my grandmother's example, I began to rejoice even in my hard circumstances.

"Praise the name of Jesus," my grandma often sang. Jesus was her rock, her fortress, her deliverer and help whom she trusted. Grandma had lived enough years without him to know how hard life was that way. She'd also lived enough years with him to know he was everything she needed, and she rejoiced in that.

My grandma's dementia got slightly worse, but we adjusted. In the course of a day she forgot she had just eaten lunch. She forgot what month it was. She forgot she had just watched a movie and asked to watch it again. But the one thing she didn't forget was Jesus, and as she remembered God her heart filled with rejoicing.

"Grandma, why do you love Jesus so much?" I asked her the other day as we sat on the front porch, enjoying the morning together.

"I love him because he first loved me. He blesses me with a new day. I start my day with him. I end my day with him. Through the night he watches over me. And he's put me into your loving care."

Grumbling comes naturally; being thankful and rejoicing do not.

"Complaining affects us. It shames us. It exposes us," wrote Ronnie Martin. "It humbles us. It reveals the hardness of our hearts. It narrows our focus to rest only on ourselves. It blinds us to who God is and to what our true needs are."[1]

And that's what not grumbling did for me. It turned my heart to God. It focused me on him. It bound me to who he is, helping me discover my true need was him. And thankfully it taught my kids the same things.

Reflection Questions

1. When has making a commitment changed everything in your life?
2. How does grumbling make your heart weak and gratitude make your heart strong?
3. What does it mean to live enough years without God to know how hard life is that way, and to live enough years with him to know he is everything we need?

Your Turn

Have you taken this grumble-free challenge? How have you done? What about your family? Take some time to write down the growth you've seen in your family. Also write down prayers of commitment to keep working toward God's best, even though the obstacles are there and the journey is long.

Stopping grumbling isn't something we can completely overcome in a year. Don't we wish! Yet if we keep our minds and our hearts focused on change, change will come. And in the words of Miss Cindy, the tae kwon do coach:

- Never give up.
- Whatever you start you must finish.
- Have a good heart and have a good mind.

Chapter 20

THE GREATEST REWARD

From the very first day that we talked about the Grumble-Free Year with our kids, we also spoke of our celebration to come at the end of our year. John and I knew what we were asking was a large undertaking. We knew our children would need a motive to work hard. We knew this reward had to be big enough—looming in the distance—to catch and hold our children's attention for the year. That's why we came up with the idea of a celebration cruise.

We never believed that taking a cruise with all these children would be a vacation. Just planning a picnic at the park is a major undertaking—how much more so to pack up ten people for five days at sea? Yet what we'd learned in our years of parenting is that, while parents should never bribe their children, we'd do well to offer more rewards for good effort. John and I both work hard to receive paychecks. We set personal goals, keeping the reward in mind, even if it is just a cleaned-off desk or looser-fitting jeans.

More than that, we understand God also knows the value of asking his children to look ahead and fix our eyes on a goal.

As Philippians 3:14 says, "I press on to reach the end of the race and receive the heavenly prize for which God, through Christ Jesus, is calling us" (NLT). A cruise couldn't compare to our heavenly reward, but it had been a great incentive for our family . . . not that I had been perfect in presenting it as a reward without turning it into a threat.

I clearly remember one day when my thirteen-year-old wouldn't stop grumbling. This came after days of "working" with her. We'd said our key Scripture verse together. We'd written notes of thankfulness and put them in the Gratitude Jar. We'd talked (I'd lectured) about grumbling words coming from a discontented heart, but none of my efforts seemed to make a difference. And then the words were out of my mouth before I could pull them back. "Don't you want to go on the cruise? If so, you better stop that grumbling now, or you're going to be the one sitting at home!"

Yes, the words came from frustration, and deep down I knew I wouldn't leave her home, but even though I saw the cruise as a reward rather than something to threaten taking away, I also enjoyed the small amount of power it gave me. Better act good or you're not going to get the big prize at the end.

And then somewhere in the middle of our year, the cruise no longer became a thing. Yes, we still planned on going, and yes, my children understood it was associated with the Grumble-Free Year, but in the midst of some very difficult days, the practice of being thankful instead of grumbling became the reward itself. Somewhere between the late nights of caregiving and the devotional moments of writing out our prayers, the hope found in God became the focus, not the bad habit we were attempting to break or the good habit we were attempting to replace it with.

This change in perspective reminded me of the change in my mind, heart, and attitude concerning my devotional time. From the time I was a young mom with three little kids, I made it a habit to wake up before them to read the Bible, pray, and journal. I have notebook after notebook of meaningful Scripture verses, prayer requests, and ramblings, and for so long I saw that time as something important on my to-do list, something that would help me understand more about God and his mandates for the way I lived.

It was only many years later, during one of my mornings, that I felt God's Spirit stirring inside me. Even though it wasn't an audible voice, I felt his Spirit saying, "Now that you know more about me, are you ready to connect with me?" And like a light bulb being flipped on in my mind, I suddenly understood the whole point of my time with Jesus: it was Jesus. It wasn't what I could learn to become a better person, but it was my soul connecting with Jesus himself and his Spirit in me preparing me for the day's walk. And not only preparing me but walking beside me.

Psalm 62:5 speaks to this truth: "My soul, wait in silence for God only, for my hope is from Him" (NASB). And that was truly the reward I desired for my children at the end of this year. Yes, we were still going on the cruise. Yes, we were still going to have fun and celebrate this year of growth, pain, trust, and thankfulness together. But I knew the hope my family and I had found in Jesus, even after a hard year, was truly the greatest reward.

Yet the greatest reward came with other small ones too. Noticeable ones.

It was the end of the Grumble-Free Year, and the Goyers were again on a road trip. This time it was to Mobile, Alabama, where we would be catching our ship to take us to Mexico. Road trips always bring conflict. After all, we are shoving a ton of people into a very small space for a long period of time.

We stopped at a gas station two hours from home for a restroom break. I looked around and noticed Maddie and Grace had already gone back to the car. The other kids picked up snacks and drinks, and when the teens saw their siblings coming out of the store with goodies, I imagined a problem: grumbling, lots of grumbling. And we were only a few hours from home.

"What about us?" Grace asked.

"We'll get something for you at the next stop," I said, eager to get back on the road.

"Oh, okay."

"We'll share!" the younger ones piped up.

I almost paused my steps as I listened to this interaction. This was yet another moment that previously would have exploded into complaining, arguing, and fights.

We all piled back into the van, and I praised all the kids for the way they handled the situation.

"We are sharing. Look!" Sissy called out.

"Yes, they really are," Maddie chimed in. Both teens had smiles on their faces, and they almost seemed surprised by my praise—as if it was obvious that was the way they should act. Maybe it had been obvious before we'd started the year, but it hadn't been a habit.

Our big family may have on the surface decided to go through a year without grumbling because it sounded like a worthy project, but I knew even more so the truth was that we were all tired of the grumbling, even those—especially those?—who were grumbling the most.

I know I was.

"Wouldn't it be nice to be appreciated for all that I do around here?" I used to comment to myself with a huff. But those moments of discontent and frustration simply fueled my own negative thoughts. Now, after all we'd learned, it was really nice having a family that treated each other with consideration, shared, and got along. Not that it was always that way, but I noticed on our long road trip it had become more common than not.

And like another layer peeling back on my self-examination, I realized even more how much of a need we all had to just get along, to be thankful, and to appreciate each other instead of grumbling.

More than anything in life, our children needed Jesus, and they needed me to model how to turn to him and allow him to transform me from the inside out and to have Jesus do the same for them. That was the only way my children would get through life with any peace, any hope. That was how they'd be able to handle all of life, the small stuff and the big stuff: with him.

As our grumble-free year moved from month to month, I understood better that while the strategies and plans I came up with were good, they weren't what made the most difference. With this project—or any project—I could have tried to manipulate my children with lots of activities, but what truly made the biggest, lasting difference was for my children to understand their need for God. They also had to seek to be changed from the inside out.

There were some things during the year that worked and some that didn't. There were times when the trials of life consumed our time, but we learned that no one walks a perfect journey and the important thing is to pause and circle back again. Together we were coming to the place where there was more peace, more thankfulness, and less grumbling in our home. And as the year drew to an end, I knew a few things:

Our family wasn't the only one that struggled with grumbling.

"Not grumbling" was something all members of the family could work on together, even if their grumbling styles and habits were different.

Grumbling was ultimately a heart issue. A heart issue only God could fix.

Parenting was all about training our children. Sometimes we worked so hard at the big stuff, like overcoming anger or deciding on the right schooling choices for our family, that we forgot about the little stuff, like grumbling. But when we focused on these heart issues—which put up a wall between us and God—we could make a lasting impact in their lives.

My kids may have hoped to gain a cruise, but the greater reward was digging out the root of the discontentment in their hearts—in all of our hearts. We're not a perfect family. We will never be a perfect family. But our year showed us that we can decide to work together for transformation. To be grateful instead of grumbling and to be thankful from deep in our hearts. The challenge was worth the change.

Reflection Questions

1. In what ways is giving our children the motivation to work hard important?

2. How have your attempts to have gratitude, instead of grumbling, given you a change of perspective?
3. In what ways are you turning toward God for transformation?

Your Turn

Take notice of the changes you've seen within your heart and within your family. Find a way to celebrate together.

TIME TO CELEBRATE

While most of our family eagerly anticipated going on our celebratory cruise trip, the idea brought a lot of anxiety for two of our kids. Both Grace and Sissy asked numerous questions. "What happens if there is a storm?" "Are there enough lifeboats for everyone?" "What if we get sick? Will there be a doctor on board?"

We tried to answer the questions as best we could, yet still they continued. As the time of our cruise grew closer, the questions turned into what appeared to be grumbles. "Why do we have to go?" "Why do we have to drive so far?" "I don't want to go on a ship. You can't make me. I'm just staying home."

Previously this would have frustrated me, but I've learned this year to pay attention to what's really going on behind the grumbles. In the case of the two girls, it was fear. Grace and Sissy liked routine. They liked to know exactly what was going to happen and when it was going to happen. The idea of leaving dry land and setting out on a new adventure with a different routine and new situations was scary, not fun.

Even on the ship, as we sat down at an elegantly set table, Grace gripped the table's edge as her voice rose in panic. "Mom, shoot me some scriptures right now!" she called out. She glanced out the window at the waves lapping the side of the ship. "I don't know if I can make it through dinner."

"Grace . . ." I fixed my gaze on hers. "Look down at your wrist."

She glanced down at the plastic bracelet all of us wore. *Grumble-Free. I can do all through him.* Grace released a heavy breath. "I can do all through Jesus. I can make it through dinner without fear. I can do all . . ."

As a family we'd set out not to grumble, but the methods we learned applied to so much more. We'd learned to turn to God when we felt like grumbling, but we'd also learned to turn to him when we were struggling with anxiety and fear. We'd learned to turn to him for strength.

Grace's ability to use scripture in the middle of an anxious moment proved that.

During the year we didn't memorize as many Scripture verses as I'd planned, but the ones we did memorize stuck, and God's Word never returns void. When God's Word is planted in our hearts, it helps us, guides us, and empowers us when we need it most.

"I can do all things . . . ," Grace whispered as her anxiety dissipated into calm.

※

One of our goals on the cruise was to share with others about our grumble-free journey, which was why we brought enough

Grumble-Free bracelets to share. Okay, my real goal was to bring the bracelets and give them to Alexis to pass out. While I tend to keep to myself, Alexis is the most outgoing person I've ever met.

A few days into the trip, I handed her a bag of Grumble-Free bracelets. "Here, can you pass these out for me?"

Excitement filled her face. "To who?"

"To the waitstaff, to the friends you made, to adults . . . anyone."

"Okay!" She bounced up and down, eager to start. She began with our waiters. "My mom is writing a book called *The Grumble-Free Year*. Our whole family worked not to grumble for a year."

Each of them asked more questions about how we did that. Alexis and some of the other kids filled them in. They seemed impressed.

But my favorite response was one Alexis told me about later.

"Mommy, I met a man at breakfast and gave him a bracelet. He asked what a grumble-free year was, and I told him. He asked if he could have bracelets for his wife and kids. He said he wanted to try a grumble-free year."

"Oh, how many kids did he have on the cruise?"

"I asked him that," Alexis said with a grin, "and he said he had two kids at home, but he didn't bring them on the cruise because they grumbled too much."

We both laughed at that, even though it really wasn't funny. It was proof that grumbling really could—and does—create a wedge (and sometimes the Gulf of Mexico) between parents and kids.

Less than twenty-four hours after I handed my daughter the bag of bracelets, all of them were passed out, and when I asked what the most common response was, Alexis grinned. It was "Congratulations!" People were quick to celebrate with her—with our whole family—not just for embarking on the journey, but also for attempting it.

The wonderful thing about the cruise was that we all walked with a lighter step, knowing we'd worked hard together. And there were a few moments that made us laugh together. First, Grace did get her own bed, as promised. Second, there was a Build-A-Bear party that our youngest kids were able to attend . . . without waiting in line for ten hours. Instead, they got to have fun with other kids and come out with fully stuffed bears in less than an hour. But the best part for me were the numerous times when I'd hear the smallest complaint and I'd simply have to say, "That wasn't a grumble, was it?"

"No, sorry. Uh, no reason to grumble," I'd hear, and I knew my family understood that grumbling had no place on our celebration cruise, and hopefully it would have less and less room in the days to follow, even after our return.

And that has me now looking to the future.

Learning not to grumble has built a foundation for my children to stand on for whatever they face in life. But grumbling is just the beginning. What other areas can we work on: worry, fear, teasing? Each family's list will be different.

It's time to ask: What do I really want for my children? What qualities do I want them to develop? Truly, none of us can have a deep, meaningful relationship with God and others without thankfulness, trust, peace, joy. *The Grumble-Free Year* is just the beginning.

We decided to end our last month memorizing these verses and talking about what other things God has called us to live out, one day at a time.

- "Therefore do not be anxious about tomorrow, for tomorrow will be anxious for itself. Sufficient for the day is its own trouble" (Matt. 6:34 ESV).

- "Delight yourself in the LORD, and he will give you the desires of your heart" (Ps. 37:4 ESV).
- "For I know the plans I have for you, declares the LORD, plans for welfare and not for evil, to give you a future and a hope" (Jer. 29:11 ESV).
- "For God gave us a spirit not of fear but of power and love and self-control" (2 Tim. 1:7 ESV).
- "You make known to me the path of life; in your presence there is fullness of joy; at your right hand are pleasures forevermore" (Ps. 16:11 ESV).

Then, when we are done, we'll see what all of us want to work on next . . .

ACKNOWLEDGMENTS

This book wouldn't be possible if my kids didn't grumble so much . . . or if I didn't either! Yet one of our biggest attitude problems became a catalyst for change. So I guess I can be thankful for that. Kids, you did a great job deciding to change and working hard for it.

I'm also thankful that my husband, John, has been available for late-night chats as we've worked through these grumble-free challenges together. I'm thankful for our adult kids, Cory and Leslie, who watched and gave us input from afar. I'm thankful for Nathan for walking this journey with us. And for Grandma, who journeyed with us too . . . even during the times she forgot what we were so intent on. Her worshipful heart during hard times was a turning point.

And I cannot give enough thanks to my agent, Janet Grant, my editor, Jessica Wong, and the amazing team at Nelson Books who made this book possible. Janet and Jessica's enthusiasm for this project gave me strength even on hard days.

Mostly I'm thankful for Jesus, who walks with us through every challenge, especially this one!

NOTES

Chapter 1: Perfectly Imperfect
1. Adele Ahberg Calhoun, *Invitations from God: Accepting God's Offer to Rest, Weep, Forgive, Wait, Remember, and More* (Westmont, IL: IVP Books, 2011).

Chapter 3: It's Time to Thrive, Not Just Survive, as a Family
1. Daniel J. Siegel and Tina Payne Bryson, *The Whole-Brain Child* (New York: Random House, 2011), 139.

Chapter 4: Let's Talk About Grumbling
1. Sam Crabtree, *Practicing Affirmation* (Wheaton, IL: Crossway, 2011), 19–20.

Chapter 7: When Life Gets in the Way of Our Plans
1. Rick Warren, "Life: A Lesson in Love," posted on OnePlace, March 2, 2017, https://www.oneplace.com/ministries/daily-hope/read/devotionals/daily-hope-with-rick-warren/life-a-lesson-in-love-daily-hope-with-rick-warren-march-2-2017-11769364.html.

Chapter 8: What Really Matters
1. Max Lucado, *God Came Near: God's Perfect Gift* (Nashville: Thomas Nelson, 2004), 4.

Chapter 9: Praise Hardwired

1. S. D. Gordon, *Quiet Talks on Prayer* (UK: Echo Library, 2007), 12.

Chapter 10: Mindful Decisions

1. Jim Stovall, *Ultimate Hindsight: Wisdom from 100 Super Achievers* (Shippensburg, PA: Sound Wisdom, 2015).

Chapter 12: Lost in the Middle of Ingratitude

1. Oswald Chambers, "Will You Lay Down Your Life?" *My Utmost for His Highest*, accessed February 28, 2019, https://utmost.org /will-you-lay-down-your-life/.

Chapter 13: Prayer Makes a Difference

1. S. D. Gordon, *Quiet Talks on Prayer* (UK: Echo Library, 2007), 2.

Chapter 15: For the Fame

1. Joanna Weaver, *Lazarus Awakening* (Colorado Springs, CO: WaterBrook Press, 2012), 146.
2. Phyllis Theroux, "Amazing Grace," *Washington Post*, October 18, 1981, https://www.washingtonpost.com/archive/lifestyle/magazine /1981/10/18/amazing-grace/80c3d328-1270-4f50-90d8 -ba72dc903b90/?noredirect=on&utm_term=.3c3807d513b9.

Chapter 18: The Day That Could Have Changed Everything

1. Jamie Ivey, "The Happy Hour #202: Brittany Price Brooker," *The Happy Hour with Jamie Ivey*, July 18, 2018, https://jamieivey.com /the-happy-hour-202-brittany-price-brooker.
2. John Piper, "Do All Things Without Grumbling," *Desiring God*, June 1, 1994, https://www.desiringgod.org/articles/do-all-things -without-grumbling.

Chapter 19: Self-Discipline and Heart Changes

1. Ronnie Martin, *Stop Your Complaining: From Grumbling to Gratitude* (Fort Washington, PA: CLC Publications, 2015), 109.

ABOUT THE
AUTHOR

Tricia Goyer is a busy mom of ten, grandmother of many, and wife to John. Somewhere around the hustle and bustle of family life, she manages to find the time to write novels and nonfiction. A *USA Today* bestselling author, Tricia has published over seventy books and is a two-time Carol Award winner, as well as a Christy and ECPA Award Finalist. Tricia won the Retailer's Best Award in 2015 and has received starred reviews from *Romantic Times* and *Publishers Weekly*. Tricia is also on the blogging team at TheBetterMom.com and other homeschooling and Christian sites. Tricia is the founder of Hope Pregnancy Ministries and currently leads a teen MOPS group in Little Rock, Arkansas.